Ministry
with
Remarried
Persons

Ministry with Remarried Persons

Richard P. Olson and
Carole Della Pia-Terry

Judson Press ® Valley Forge

MINISTRY WITH REMARRIED PERSONS

Library of Congress Cataloging in Publication Data

Olson, Richard P.
  Ministry with remarried persons.

  1. Church work with remarried people.
I. Della Pia-Terry, Carole.   II. Title.
BV4439.O47 1984   259   83-26827
ISBN 0-8170-0990-6

Contents

A Note from the Authors

This book is one volume of a two-volume effort to contribute to the church's ministry with remarried couples and families. The other volume, entitled *Help for Remarried Couples and Families,* is directed to remarried persons and those planning to be remarried. This one is prepared for ministers and church leaders who are now working with (or are planning to work with) remarried couples and families.

Both volumes are the result of partnership in writing. One of the partners, Carole, is a divorcée remarried to a widower. She is a mother and a stepmother. She has studied this subject widely and has brought her own firsthand knowledge and the results of many conversations and intensive interviews to her writing task. The other partner, Dick, is a pastor, husband, and father. He has brought his discipline of pastoral care and his experience in working with many remarried families to his task of writing.

In *Help for Remarried Couples and Families* Carole's rich experience and knowledge is clearly shared at many points, and this wisdom is combined with Dick's reflections. So most of that volume uses the pronoun "we" to indicate shared viewpoints.

When it came to writing this volume, Carole and Dick readily agreed that Dick had the expertise to speak to church leaders. So in this book Dick has explored the implications for church leaders of the issues raised in *Help for Remarried Couples and Families.* In doing so, he often uses the pronoun "I". He speaks only for himself when he does that, for Carole does not speak as a church leader. However, since the real experts on the subject of remarriage are those who have survived and grown in their own remarriages, Carole's experiences and viewpoints are clearly shared, citing her by name. We hope this clarifies who "Carole" and "I" are in these pages and prepares you to share this pilgrimage, exploring together an opportunity for ministry.

A Pastoral Theology of Remarriage

The question of remarriage is really the question of the relevancy of the Christian faith. . . . As Karl Heim has put it, "The church's future today depends more than ever on whether [it] withdraws into the ghetto and leaves the world to its fate, or whether [it] has the authority to continue the discussion with the world outside and to answer the question which it puts to [it]."—James G. Emerson, Jr.[1]

The new embarrassment is that the Church cannot minister to the divorced in [its] midst because [its] theology of divorce and remarriage has been found wanting.—Dwight Hervey Small[2]

The institution of marriage was ordained by God to be a permanent, enduring association between a man and a woman, and ideally it should last till the death of one spouse dissolves it. However, permanency and indissolubility are not to be confused. —Victor Pospishil[3]

"I feel God is a realist." —said by a divorced person and recalled by G. Edwin Bontrager[4]

More than twenty years ago, when I was a theological student studying the ethical teachings of Jesus, one thing seemed quite clear to me: Jesus forbade divorce and remarriage. Oh, I understood that many things Jesus called us to do were "kingdom-ethic"—instructions to live in the "future" kingdom of God right now. I recognized that some of his claims were beyond the capabilities of poor struggling Christian believers right now, but Jesus' kingdom commands about divorce and remarriage seemed to me to be reasonable and manageable. I felt that even though I might not be able to obey perfectly all the kingdom commands, I could and would keep that one command.

At the same time, I realized that I was being helped by the gifts and kindness of two people, both single. The woman was divorced because her husband had become mentally ill and had sometimes attacked her, nearly strangling her. The man was single because his wife had gone to a different climate for her health. When the crisis in her health passed, she refused to come back. I had no knowledge whether the estranged spouses of these two people fell into either of the New Testament's two "escape clauses" involving adulterers or unbelievers. But I believed that both of my friends were innocent. I was happy for them when I heard that they had been divorced from their previous spouses and had married each other. I hoped that they would have much happiness together and that in their new life together they would experience healing after long years of suffering and loneliness.

Even before I started serving a pastorate, my view had changed a bit: I would be faithful to Jesus' teaching and officiate only at weddings of the previously unmarried, the widowed, and the *innocently* divorced.

It did not take long for me as a pastor to discover the fallacy of that view, for those who frequently confronted me were not people who wanted my advice about staying together versus divorce. Rather, they were people who had divorced, had decided to remarry someone else, and wanted my assistance as pastor to participate in a wedding. They were seeking God's blessing on their union. It was impossible to determine whether I was talking to the "innocent" parties. (It is unlikely that there is ever an "innocent" party and a "guilty" party in marital discord.) Usually I did not know the divorced spouses. I heard only the side of the story presented by the persons in my office. No matter how hard they tried to be fair, what they told was from their perspective. I could not be sure whether I was doing the right thing. The role of "judge" was a most uncomfortable one for me indeed. I had entered the ministry to console, to offer support and care, to witness to the God of love. Judging—deciding whether or not I would officiate at the wedding of a particular couple—was a distasteful task for me. I fear that for some time I was indecisive and ambivalent. Whether I participated in a previously divorced couple's wedding or not, I was not as much help to them as I might have been.

As far as I could tell, some other clergy persons were even less responsive than I, and so couples lacked pastoral counsel and support at this most important time in their lives. Consider:

—the couple (one partner was divorced) who were told that they could not be married in the sanctuary but could be married in the "chapel" (actually an overflow room which would not have provided space for a dignified service), or they could rent some other church building. They chose to go elsewhere.

—the couple who, as divorced singles, had been participating faithfully in a church that had contributed to their Christian awakening and growth. Their pastor told them that he would not officiate at their wedding. If they could find a clergy who would perform the ceremony, they could continue coming to his church, the church they had been attending. They could sing in the choir but could *not* sing solos; they could *not* be deacon or deaconness (church officers) or church school teachers. Since they loved to do all those things, they rejected second-class membership and went elsewhere.

—the divorced woman who called her pastor to tell him that her wedding (her second) would not be at the church but at the office of the justice of the peace "because it will be less bothersome to you and the church."

—the divorced and remarried woman who told her former priest, "I didn't leave my church; my church left me!"

These examples suggest that much of the church perceives remarrying people as sinners beyond the pale. In Karl Heim's words, "The church has withdrawn into a ghetto, leaving the world of remarrying people to their own fate."[5]

Well, to continue the story, in time I worked out a style of ministry on this remarriage matter with which I could live, a style that took seriously Jesus' high regard for marriage as well as his gospel of love, grace, and forgiveness. Though I did not have my approach worked out as thoughtfully as I am attempting to do now, my basic response when asked, "Do you officiate at the weddings of divorced persons?" was "Yes, but never casually."

So I participated in a number of these remarriage ceremonies and attempted to provide ongoing pastoral care to these persons and their families. During this time I happened on another discovery, actually a double discovery: the issue of remarriage will become more persistent as the divorce rate soars (it has already soared from 25 percent to 33 percent to 40 percent), and many persons in these remarriages have a difficult time making a go of it. I am told that a basic rule of thumb is that two-thirds of first marriages remain intact; one-half of second marriages survive, and one-third of third marriages do so! What the pastor needs to develop is not merely a theory of divorce and remarriage; if he or she chooses to participate in such weddings, he or she also

needs a theological perspective and strategy to help the marriages
survive, even though they may encounter extra pitfalls that threaten
their permanent survival.

To sum up, my circumstances as a clergy in this matter are something
like this:

—I face an ethical issue: officiating with increasing frequency at the
remarriages of divorced and/or widowed people.

—I have an uneasy conscience and some unresolved questions about
doing so.

—This unease and lack of perspective on my part may get in the
way of my ability to minister as completely as possible. Research to
date indicates that a remarrying couple may have the greatest need
for assistance in establishing a permanent, meaningful union.

This combination of circumstances suggests that, as a clergyperson, I
ought to get my act together.

When I discuss this issue with my fellow clergy and observe their
behavior, I see a variety of responses to this issue. Some clergy say,
"My ecclesiastical superiors have made decisions that I am obligated
to follow. I have little or no room for personal decision making." Other
clergy say, "The teaching of Jesus is clear. He forbade divorce and
remarriage. So I refuse to participate in any marriage in which one
partner has been divorced." As a slight variation to this theme, some
clergy say, "Yes, Jesus forbade divorce and remarriage, but the Bible
does allow for two exceptions: if a spouse is unfaithful (Matthew 19:3-
9) and if an unbelieving spouse initiates the divorce (1 Corinthians
7:12-16). If either of these two circumstances has occurred, I will
officiate at the wedding. If not, I simply cannot. This may seem harsh
and force me to turn away some very nice people, but it also dams this
flood of divorces and remarriages. It is kinder to society in the long
run."

Other clergy say, "I just trust that the couple has worked out these
problems with their God. If they want to be remarried, I officiate at
their wedding. I rarely raise questions or discuss the biblical teachings
about marriage with the couples who come to me." And still other
clergy say, "I view those biblical teachings as archaic, given our present
society. I try to respond situationally, as a loving person. Today there
is much divorce and remarriage. Maybe that's a good thing. Perhaps
lifelong commitments are unrealistic any more. At any rate, my response
is supportive, caring, individual, and situational."

I find myself uneasy with all of the above approaches and desire a more thorough and thoughtful pastoral theology to inform me as I make my decisions in this arena.

I attempt to construct this theology by carrying on a dialogue with the biblical material from my place in contemporary society. I do this as one who takes biblical teachings—and especially the teachings of Jesus—very seriously. Thus, I need to ask four questions to help me formulate a pastoral theology of divorce and remarriage.

1. What is the Old Testament teaching on marriage-divorce-remarriage, the background against which we see the teachings of Jesus?
2. What are the nature and content of Jesus' ethical teachings?
3. What are the nature and content of Jesus' teachings on marriage-divorce-remarriage?
4. In my social situation and with my pastoral opportunities, how do I become more faithful to the discoveries that I make as a result of answering the previous three questions?

Let's consider these questions in turn.

The Background/Antecedents of Jesus' Teachings (Marriage-Divorce-Remarriage in the Old Testament)

The Old Testament is a huge collection of diverse literature reflecting the story of a people living in a covenant with their God for many centuries. It is, therefore, difficult to offer a concise summary of Old Testament teachings on marriage. Still, I will make an attempt.

It seems to me that there are four themes in the Old Testament on the subject of marriage-divorce-remarriage. The first theme is that marriage was created by divine intention. In the Bible's first statement on marriage (Genesis 2:18-24), the creation of the sexes is seen as God's response to the human need for community. God declared, "It is not good that man should be alone," and first created the animals, which man named. But there was no animal fit to be a companion. Then God created woman and brought the woman to the man, who exclaimed, "This at last is bone of my bones and flesh of my flesh. . . ." The passage concludes, "Therefore a man leaves his father and his mother and cleaves to his wife, and they become one flesh" (Genesis 2:23-24).

The concise term "one flesh" contains the basic content of the divine intention for marriage. R. Lofton Hudson suggests that this phrase "one flesh" refers to "two people living together in mutual respect, love, growth, and helpfulness. . . . It is spiritual and emotional. . . . It is more the feeling-flow between two people."[6] Paul Eppinger notes that while some take the phrase "one flesh" to be an image for sexual intercourse, others think it communicates much more than that. "It really connotes the total meaning of intimacy, i.e., the interrelating of two individuals emotionally, spiritually, mentally, psychologically and physically, and thus formed the original basic purpose of marriage."[7] And Joe Leonard observes that "one flesh" also implies separation from the family of origin and commitment to the founding of a new marital union and family.[8] In the Genesis passage, then, marriage is seen as an intimate relationship in which each of two people finds satisfaction and fulfillment in what is clearly willed by God to be a lifelong exclusive commitment, one to the other.

The second theme is that marriage quite clearly had a variety of purposes. Some of these purposes caused marriage to fall short of the lofty ideal of "one flesh." Paul Eppinger, examining the biblical material, has located five other purposes or functions of marriage in the Old Testament:

1. In the patriarchal period (approximately 2000–1700 B.C.), the key purpose of marriage was to *assure immortality to the man* through the *begetting* of *male children* who would carry on his name. This concept had its roots in God's promise to Abram that God would make of Abram's descendents a great nation. Sterility and childlessness therefore became great catastrophes in a marriage. A number of steps were taken to deal with childlessness: the husband might have married more wives; his wife might have offered her female servants to him to bear children on her behalf.

This purpose of marriage also led to the custom called "levirate marriages," in which a man was expected to impregnate the widow of his dead brother, if the couple had been childless, so that his deceased brother's name might be continued. Clearly, if immortality through childbearing becomes the key purpose of marriage, the one-flesh ideal is diminished.

2. During the period of the monarchy (1020–586 B.C.), one purpose of marriage among royalty was to *increase political power* and to *form political alliances*—in short, political expediency. For example, in 1 Samuel 18:17, King Saul gave David a daughter in marriage and told him ". . . but in return you must serve me valiantly and fight the Lord's battles." Another example was King Solomon, who married Pharaoh's daughter. The account further tells us that he had seven hundred wives

who were princesses (1 King 9:16; 11:1-3). Political-alliance marriages are also unlikely to fit the one-flesh ideal.

3. During the same period, marriage for the common citizen might well have had an *economic purpose*. In the semi-nomadic and agricultural periods of Israel's history, obtaining several wives, each of whom might bear many children, would assure a man a large work force to tend the flocks and care for the fields. If marriage was a political expediency for the kings, it appeared to be an economic expediency for the male citizen.

4. When we examine the writing prophets (760–560 B.C.), we find that only two speak of their own marriages and families and both of them seem to see their families simply as *extensions of their prophetic messages*. This use of family as an extension of prophetic message was seen in the naming of children. Isaiah named his sons *Shearjashub*, which translates "a remnant shall return" (Isaiah 7:3), and *Maher-shalal-hash-baz*, which translates "speed-spoil-hasten-plunder" (Isaiah 8:1). The other prophet, Hosea, spoke of his unhappy marriage as an example of Israel's unfaithfulness to God. He named three children, probably born over a period of at least six years, to reflect his message of betrayal and doom. The children were named *Jezreel*, "God shall sow" (Hosea 1:4), *Lo-ruhamah*, "Not pitied" (1:6), and *Lo-ami*, "Not my people" (1:8). Eppinger concludes that since the prophets offered no other mention of their family lives, they did not regard marriage as the opportunity for that one-flesh, intimate relationship with another person; rather, they seemed to see marriage as simply an extension of their all-consuming prophetic messages. This may be too sweeping a conclusion, but our only evidence points in this direction.

5. One other purpose of marriage in Old Testament literature is noted: *the maintaining and perpetuating of a covenant people*. This theme is clearly seen in the story of Ezra, who, when he returned from exile, learned that Israelites had intermarried with "the peoples of the lands with their abominations" (Ezra 9:1). He reported his response: "When I heard this, I rent my garments and my mantle, and pulled hair from my head and beard, and sat appalled" (9:3). He immediately fasted, prayed, and then commanded, "Separate yourselves from the peoples of the land and from the foreign wives" (9:11). The subsequent story makes clear that this process of securing the divorce of Israelites from persons of the surrounding nations was carried out. Eppinger notes this as a day when a leader perceived God commanding divorce.[9] The purpose of marriage here was the procreation of pure Israelites for the

upbuilding of the covenant people. If a marriage would not contribute
to that end (even, if it was a one-flesh marriage) it had to be terminated.

The witness is clear that the purposes and functions of marriage in
Old Testament times were in addition to the lofty ideal of Genesis 2.

The third theme we note in the Old Testament is that divorce was a
social issue in the culture. Myrna and Robert Kysar note that divorce
and remarriage are mentioned in a number of different kinds of passages.
(a) There are legislative passages that dictate regulations for daughters
of priests who have been divorced (Leviticus 22:13) and for women
who have been seduced or slandered (Deuteronomy 22:19, 28-29).
Another passage forbids priests to marry divorced women (Leviticus
21:14). (b) There is also a prophetic passage (Malachi 2:13-16) that
notes with alarm the frequency of divorce among the Hebrew people.
Malachi declares that divorce is an insult to God because it is so easy
to obtain, and further, that divorce is objectionable because it inflicts
cruelty upon women. (c) There are many metaphorical passages in
which divorce is used to illustrate the relationship of God to the people
of Israel (for example Jeremiah 3:1-8, Isaiah 50:1, and Hosea 1-3).

All these references to divorce lead the Kysars to conclude that
divorce was a rather common practice and was culturally acknowledged
in Hebrew society. Divorce was common enough to be an easily recognized metaphor, to require humanizing legislation, and to outrage
some sensitive prophetic voices.[10]

The fourth theme is the search for a greater degree of justice in
marriage and divorce. In particular, there is the tendency toward greater
protection of the rights of women, who were the powerless ones in this
society and certainly were the persons with fewer rights in divorce.[11]
We discover this in the brief statements made about divorce in the law
passages of the Old Testament, even though, surprisingly enough, no
general legislation addressed the issues of divorce and remarriage.

The most basic passage of law about divorce and remarriage is
Deuteronomy 24:1-4:

> "When a man takes a wife and marries her, if then she finds no favor
> in his eyes because he has found some indecency in her, and he writes
> her a bill of divorce and puts it in her hand and sends her out of his house,
> and she departs out of his house, and if she goes and becomes another
> man's wife, and the latter husband dislikes her and writes her a bill of
> divorce and puts it in her hand and sends her out of his house, or if the
> latter husband dies, who took her to be his wife, then her former husband,
> who sent her away, may not take her again to be his wife, after she has
> been defiled; for that is an abomination before the LORD, and you shall

not bring guilt upon the land which the Lord your God gives you for an inheritance.''

When we read this passage carefully, we discover that its ruling is that a twice-divorced woman may not be taken back by her first husband.

A more detailed summary comes out looking something like this:

IF
—a man does not find his wife in his favor because he has found "some indecency in her,"and
—he writes her a bill of divorcement, presents it to her (presumably in the presence of witnesses), sends her out of the house, and she leaves, and
—she marries again, and
—her second husband also divorces her or dies,
THEN
—the first husband may not take her back
BECAUSE
—this is an abomination to the Lord and brings guilt upon the land.

This very complete statement on divorce, then, makes a rather technical point about remarriage to a former spouse. The reason for this legislation is not given except that remarrying a former spouse in an abomination to the Lord.

In moving to this point, however, the passage makes some assumptions and describes the prevailing divorce practice. It was this practice that was raised in discussion with Jesus centuries later, a discussion we will shortly note. With a fair degree of confidence we can extract from the passage in Deuteronomy what, in the law of Moses, was to be the fair and just divorce procedure:

1. The man had to have some grounds for divorce. The phrase "if then she finds no favor in his eyes because he has found some indecency in her" (Deuteronomy 24:2) refers to those grounds for divorce. Unfortunately, it is not clear what this phrase meant. The Hebrew phrase translated "some indecency" literally means "the nakedness of a thing."[12] Students and scholars in the centuries since have suggested that it may have meant committing adultery, burning the food that they were to eat, or simply losing her appeal to her husband. The Mishnah interpreted the phrase to mean that the woman had broken the law or custom or influenced her husband to do so.[13] These grounds for divorce seem extremely vague, but there had to have been some.

2. When some ground for divorce occurred, the man could (not, as some earlier translations seem to say, the man *had to*) divorce her. He did this by writing a formal bill of divorcement, probably signed by witnesses and delivered in the presence of witnesses.

3. When he sent her out of the house, she left.

4. Implied in these steps was a settlement in regard to the dowry. Though there was no uniform practice in settling this matter, a fairly well accepted Jewish practice in later Jewish history was that the husband returned his wife's dowry, plus an equivalent sum from his own estate. Thus economic considerations might well have slowed down the impulse to divorce or prohibited it.[14]

5. When the husband took these steps, the wife was free to remarry and so was he, presumably.

6. However, he had to realize that if she did remarry, the step was irreversable; she could never remarry him.

These procedures would have had the effect of slowing down the divorce process, preventing hasty decisions, emphasizing the importance and permanence of the step the man was taking, and requiring him to consider economic-welfare ramifications as well as personal feelings, thereby humanizing the divorce process. This, along with some rather stern legislation concerning the man who slandered his wife (Deuteronomy 22:13-19) and the man who seduced an unmarried woman and married her (Deuteronomy 22:28-29), constitutes about all we know in regard to divorce and remarriage legislation in the Old Testament.

In the legislation we are exploring, only men had the right to initiate divorce proceedings. However, documents have been discovered from the Jewish community in Egypt, dating from as early as the fifth century before Christ, which reveal that Jewish women in that community did have the right to divorce.[15]

Surprisingly, there was no general legislation concerning divorce and remarriage. But the glimpses we do have perhaps justify the conclusion with which we began to explore this theme, namely that

God is concerned in situations of divorce and remarriage, as in all situations in which humans find themselves, to protect the dignity of the powerless. If the woman may be regarded as the underdog in ancient Hebraic divorce practices—as indeed we believe she must be—then the legislation of the Torah tends to move toward siding with the underdog. That view is consistent with the totality of the concept of God found in the Old Testament.[16]

The legislation we have examined did not eliminate the oppression, but it did temper it. We thus conclude this brief survey of the Old Testament literature on marriage-divorce-remarriage with this summary:

1. The Bible affirms a deep, spiritual, permanent one-flesh union as the ideal and purpose of marriage.

2. Marriage actually served many functions, some of which interfered with the one-flesh ideal.

3. The references imply that divorce and probably remarriage were quite frequent.

4. The legislation involving divorce represented the compassion of God for the powerless and thus introduced some humanizing procedures.

The Nature of Jesus' Ethical Teachings

Before we can examine Jesus' teachings about marriage-divorce-remarriage against the background of the Old Testament, we need to pause for a moment and examine the nature of Jesus' teachings in general, for this will have a bearing on our understanding of what Jesus said about our particular subject. We will briefly summarize some of the results of biblical scholarship on the teachings of Jesus:

1. Jesus' central theme was the kingdom of God. He proclaimed that the kingdom of God burst upon people in the person and acts of Jesus and that it was coming with power.

2. Jesus invited people to respond to him as disciples and as persons who would live in the present world by the kingdom ethic, as if the kingdom had already come.

3. His ethic, therefore, is for individuals who have accepted his invitation and will attempt to live out the kingdom ethic here in this world.

4. Jesus' teachings are a kingdom ideal, a call for radical obedience, a call to challenge, and a call to live beyond the cultural norms of the day. He expected his teachings to be obeyed both in the inner person and in outer-directed behavior. In the deepest sense one will never come to the end of one's obedience to Jesus' teachings.

5. Jesus sometimes used teaching devices such as the hyperbole, which is an exaggeration or an overstatement, to stir the listener to deeper reflection.

6. Jesus gave primary concern to the person rather than to institutions. He constantly challenged the hallowed institutions of the sabbath, the Law, and the temple. He explicitly stated, "The sabbath was made for

man, not man for the sabbath'' (Mark 2:27). And we can reasonably assume that he would have given primacy to the best welfare of the person over the institution of marriage as well.

7. Jesus' teaching contains two points of focus. Myrna and Robert Kysar summarize them in this little chart:

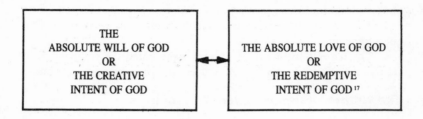

| THE ABSOLUTE WILL OF GOD OR THE CREATIVE INTENT OF GOD | THE ABSOLUTE LOVE OF GOD OR THE REDEMPTIVE INTENT OF GOD [17] |

On one hand, we hear Jesus proclaiming the absolute will of God, the radical demands of God on one's life as one serves in the kingdom of God. The call is to radical goodness, commitment, completeness. On the other hand, Jesus proclaims the absolute love of God, the radical acceptance of God. He tells about, models, and lives out an acceptance of sinners, outcasts, and the nondescript people of the land. He incarnates God's love of humanity and acceptance of all, even those who have failed. We misread Jesus if we read his statements on either side of this (that is, either the absolute will or the absolute forgiveness of God) without seeing those statements in dynamic tension with the statements on the other side.

We shall be guided by this awareness of Jesus' teaching as we examine his specific teachings on marriage-divorce-remarriage.

Jesus' Teaching on Marriage-Divorce-Remarriage

Jesus held marriage in extremely high regard. As a traditional wedding ceremony states: ''Marriage is an honorable estate, instituted of God and beautified by Jesus when he wrought his first miracle in Cana of Galilee'' (see John 2:1-11). Jesus used images of marriage to explore the nature of the kingdom that he proclaimed. The kingdom of God is like a marriage feast (Matthew 22:1-11). The urgency of the kingdom is like the wise and the foolish maidens waiting for the wedding celebration (Matthew 25:1-13). The priorities of the kingdom are like the wedding festivities described by Jesus in Mark 2:18-22.

But Jesus' clearest teachings about marriage are seen in the passages in which he speaks of divorce, either on his own initiative or under questioning. Let us place these passages before us for our examination and reflection:

Matthew 19:3-12

And the Pharisees came up to him and tested him by asking, "Is it lawful to divorce one's wife for any cause?" He answered, "Have you not read that he who made them from the beginning made them male and female, and said, 'For this reason a man shall leave his father and mother and be joined to his wife, and the two shall become one flesh'? So they are no longer two but one flesh. What therefore God has joined together, let not man put asunder." They said to him, "Why then did Moses command one to give a certificate of divorce, and to put her away?" He said to them, "For your hardness of heart Moses allowed you to divorce your wives, but from the beginning it was not so. And I say to you: whoever divorces his wife, except for unchastity, and marries another, commits adultery."

The disciples said to him, "If such is the case of a man with his wife, it is not expedient to marry." But he said to them, "Not all men can receive this saying, but only those to whom it is given. For there are eunuchs who have been so from birth, and there are eunuchs who have been made eunuchs by men, and there are eunuchs who have made themselves eunuchs for the sake of the kingdom of heaven. He who is able to receive this, let him receive it."

Mark 10:2-12

And Pharisees came up and in order to test him asked, "Is it lawful for a man to divorce his wife?" He answered them, "What did Moses command you?" They said, "Moses allowed a man to write a certificate of divorce, and to put her away." But Jesus said to them, "For your hardness of heart he wrote you this commandment. But from the beginning of creation, 'God made them male and female.' 'For this reason a man shall leave his father and mother and be joined to his wife, and the two shall become one flesh.' So they are no longer two but one flesh. What therefore God has joined together, let not man put asunder."

And in the house the disciples asked him again about this matter. And he said to them, "Whoever divorces his wife and marries another, commits adultery against her; and if she divorces her husband and marries another, she commits adultery."

Matthew 5:32

But I say to you that everyone who divorces his wife except on the ground of unchastity, makes her an adulteress; and whoever marries a divorced woman commits adultery.

Luke 16:18

"Everyone who divorces his wife and marries another commits adultery, and he who marries a woman divorced from her husband commits adultery."

In Matthew 19 and Mark 10, Jesus was questioned by Pharisees about the possibility of divorce. Scholars feel that Matthew reported their question more accurately. Since divorce was common, the Pharisees' question as quoted by Mark, " 'Is it lawful for a man to divorce his wife?' " would be like asking a politician if the president is elected every four years.[18] The question that Matthew quoted was more comprehensive: "'Is it lawful to divorce one's wife for any cause?' " In other words, "What are the acceptable grounds for divorce?"

In both situations when Jesus questioned the Pharisees, they quoted the Mosaic legislation found in Deuteronomy 24:1-4. As we have noted, there was and is widespread disagreement as to what constituted grounds for divorce, as described in that passage. Both Matthew and Mark noted that the Pharisees asked their question in a trapping, testing manner, not in the spirit of genuine inquiry. Rather, they were asking, "Whose side are you on in interpreting Deuteronomy 24:1-4? And incidentally, whatever side you take, you'll alienate someone!"

But Jesus would have none of it. He did not want to enter into minute legislative disputes. Rather, he referred to God's ultimate divine purpose in creating man and woman each for the other: when they entered into the marriage bond, they might become one flesh.

Then, after summarizing Genesis 2:21-24, he added his own word of counsel-command, "What therefore God has joined together, let not man put asunder"(Matthew 19:6b). These words (so familiar from their inclusion in the wedding service of today) do contain the recognition that "man" can disrupt the one-flesh union that God intends for a marriage. Either partner in a marriage can disrupt it, or other individuals can do so, or society/culture can make the union difficult to achieve. Jesus urged all—those within a marriage and those outside it—not to tamper with divine intention for the marital union.

The conclusion of these two accounts (Matthew 19:9 and Mark 10:11-12), along with another passage in Matthew 5:32 and one in Luke 16:18, contain strong statements from Jesus on the subject of divorce and remarriage. All make clear that Jesus believed that one does not escape the prohibitions against adultery by divorcing and remarriage. Jesus defined the process of divorcing one wife and marrying another as adultery as well.

In taking this position Jesus is stating in the starkest terms the absolute will of God, God's radical demands. Neither here nor anywhere else in the Gospels does he state the absolute love of God or the radical acceptance of God for persons unable to keep this counsel of perfection will of God, God's radical demands. Neither here nor anywhere else in the Gospels does he state the absolute love of God or the radical acceptance of God for persons unable to keep this counsel of perfection in divorce and remarriage. However, we may be sure that such assurance of God's forgiving love would have been given here as it is in other areas of the gospel.

When one examines these four recorded statements of Jesus on divorce and remarriage, one notices a striking difference among them. Both of the Matthew references include an exception clause. Jesus instructed a man not to divorce his wife, "except for unchastity, . . ." The Luke and Mark references, however, do not include this clause. Bible scholars conclude that one of four explanations must be true: (a) Jesus spoke of this on more than one occasion, sometimes mentioning the phrase "except for unchastity" and sometimes not; (b) when Jesus spoke of divorce, he used this phrase, but somehow Luke and Mark omitted it; (c) when Jesus spoke of divorce, he did not use this phrase, but perhaps Matthew (or the early Christian church) added it to tone down a command from Jesus that seemed too harsh, too impossible to achieve; or (d) the early church added the qualifying phrase to speak to problems it was encountering regularly.

No one one knows the right explanation for sure, of course, but most Bible scholars tend to favor (c); that is, Jesus' original statement was a striking, unqualified statement that included no exceptions.

Small wonder then that even Jesus' disciples, who had heard him proclaim his kingdom ethics on other subjects, were shocked. "If that is the position with husband and wife, it is better not to marry" (Matthew 19:10, NEB), they said.

And Jesus responded with what *may* have been a slight move in the direction of recognizing human weakness by saying, "Not all men can receive this saying, but only those to whom it is given." This response can be roughly translated, "Well, this command isn't for everyone." Whether he was saying that some who cannot maintain their marriage commitment should not marry or that he recognized that not all married people could keep their marriage commitment is not clear.

While the text is not explicit, many scholars feel that Jesus might have been taking such a stand out of concern that women be treated as persons. If the process prescribed in Deuteronomy 24 slowed down divorce and prevented hasty divorces that would have imposed hardship on powerless women, then Jesus took another step on their behalf when he said, "Divorce not at all." He was recognizing that when a woman was divorced (and, you recall, she had little or no right of divorce herself), she had four unhappy options: prostitution; returning to a family that possibly could not afford to feed her; starvation; or remarriage, very possibly a desperate remarriage to save her life but also one in which she had no rights. Quite possibly Jesus was saying, "Don't treat people that way!"

Up to this point, we have examined the content of Jesus' sayings on divorce and remarriage. Now we must explore an equally important question. What was the nature and character of these teachings? How do these particular teachings appear in the context of what we have said about the character of Jesus' teachings in general?

Some people read Jesus' teachings as general law that requires some further legislation on minor details, but *law*, nevertheless, to be applied in a straightforward manner. They would find the interpretation to be quite simple: either all people (or all with the exception of innocent victims of adultery—the exception clause mentioned in Matthew) may not divorce, or at least they may not remarry if they wish to remain a part of the church.

I feel those who interpret Jesus' teachings in this way are mistaken. Considering the character of his teachings in general, I think it is reasonable to agree with those scholars who say that Jesus' word about divorce and remarriage was

—a *"call to repentence"* to persons who had grown rather lax and flippant about divorce, rather than setting up a new law code.[19]

—"not a new law, but an extraordinary ethical ideal."[20]

—" a moral *ideal*, a counsel, [not] a legal norm."[21]

In their book *The Asundered* the Kysars conclude,

> These radical assertions of God's creative intention for humanity [about divorce and remarriage] found in the teachings of Jesus were never meant to be law for the Christian. Jesus' whole ministry involved an attack upon a legalism which attempted to put God's will into precise prescriptions. . . . The reign of God that Jesus announced could not be packaged. . . . We cannot then, in faithfulness to Jesus, make of his teachings a new legalism. That would be like the leaders of a rebellion overthrowing the tyranny of a nation's officials only to establish a new tyranny once they had gained power. While the teachings of Jesus vividly present the will of God for humanity, they are not a new law. To understand them that way does violence to the spirit of the prophet of Nazareth.[22]

What then do we conclude about the teaching of Jesus on marriage-divorce-remarriage? (a) Jesus affirmed in the strongest possible terms the Genesis one-flesh ideal of permanent, intimate marriage between two persons. (b) He refused to be drawn into legislating the details of this, but rather stated it as an ideal of the kingdom of God. (c) His statements against divorce and remarriage were so stark and strong, especially as seen against contemporary practice, that they may have been hyperbole—a striking exaggeration to stir careful thought, reflection, and action on the part of the listener. (d) These statements were a call to repentence, "an extraordinary ethical ideal," "a moral counsel"—not a legal norm or a new law. (e) Jesus' statements were meant to be taken seriously and obeyed whenever possible, but Jesus also proclaimed a forgiving God of love and compassion who tenderly forgives and heals those who fail. (f) Jesus always saw human need preceding institutional need, and so we believe that he would probably tell us that marriage is made for humans, not humans for marriage. (g) Quite possibly he made his original statements, in part, from the concern for the welfare of powerless women; so today he might approach this topic out of concern for the welfare of both women and men. As Robert Sinks suggests, "Whenever marriage serves to crush what is genuinely human, then it must yield to the higher principle of the Great Commandment."[23] (h) So, while never taking divorce and remarriage casually or flippantly, we may be led by the forgiving spirit of Christ in directions his words never *specifically* described.

Before concluding this discussion we should briefly mention two passages from the writings of the apostle Paul. In Romans 7:1-3 Paul argued for the dominion of law over a person's life until one "dies to sin." In this connection he used the illustration that a woman was bound to her husband as long as he lived. If he died, Paul continued, she was free to be married to another man. In a passage in which marriage and divorce simply illustrate another theme, namely the person and the law, Paul reflected the view of marriage as a permanent bond, found in the teachings of Jesus and in Genesis 2.

In 1 Corinthians 7:10-16, Paul examined the subject of marriage-divorce-remarriage more directly. In order to understand this passage, we need to know two things about the books of Corinthians: (a) these two books are a collection of Paul's letters to a troubled church that had raised many questions and issues to which he was responding directly; (b) Paul was writing with vivid expectation of the immediate return of Christ. As he stated in 1 Corinthians 7:26, ". . . in view of the present distress it is well for a person to remain as he is." He may then have been more unyielding in what he understood to be the rigorous life demanded of Christians preparing for the end.

In verses 10-11 he first summarized (and he made clear that these words were not his but the Lord's) Jesus' teaching that persons were not to separate or divorce, and if they did so, they were to remain single or be reconciled to their spouses.

In verses 12-16, first making clear that this was his own counsel, Paul addressed a problem unique to his readers' situation: what if one spouse was a believer in Christ and the other was not? His first qualification was that if the unbelieving partner was willing to remain married, the Christian partner should be willing too. But if the unbelieving partner wanted to separate, then the Christian partner should allow it. In such cases Paul said, "The brother or sister is not bound." (Some see an implication here that remarriage is allowed. It is not clear whether "not bound" means not bound to the marriage or actually free to remarry.) Then Paul added a word calling for restraint in this decision in case the believer might be instrumental in his or her partner's salvation.

Persons who read the New Testament as law find in this passage one more "exception clause." That is, possibly the divorced Christian is free to remarry (a) if she or he is the innocent party and the former spouse was involved in adultery or (b) if the former spouse was an unbeliever who initiated the divorce. Persons who read the New Testament as moral direction and not as law see this passage as indicating a new principle. Early Christians like Paul and Matthew understood the word of Jesus as guidance to be interpreted from the point of view of human welfare, not as a set of absolute rules. [24]

For those who read Paul's teaching as law, it might be well to view Paul's words on divorce and remarriage in light of his most central, most basic, teaching—that is, people do not come to a right relationship with God by merely obeying the law (old or new). Rather, people are reconciled to God through God's grace, in Christ, to which we respond in faith. [25] This is not a cheap grace that flippantly encourages easy divorce, but a costly grace speaking to people in the pain of failed marital hopes. Again, we must consider the circumstances of divorced persons seeking remarriage, not only from the point of view of the *will* of God, but also from the perspective of the *grace* of God.

How Then Do I, a Minister of the Gospel, Respond to the Divorced and Widowed Seeking Remarriage?

In light of all this biblical background and discussion, how do I as a Christian minister respond to the ever-growing number of requests that I assist persons in remarrying?

Earlier we mentioned that Jesus' teachings had two foci: the *absolute will* of God, the radical demands of God on one's life in the kingdom of God; and the *absolute love* of God, the radical acceptance by God of us in our frailty and sin. Each focus provides a perspective for the modern pastor's response to the needs of persons who are remarrying.

In regard to God's radical will for our lives, Jesus spoke against divorce in light of the one-flesh ideal articulated in Genesis 2:21-24. The more one considers this passage, the more it becomes clear that Jesus' teaching was intended to call forth a deeper understanding of marriage, not to deny the possibility of divorce.[26]

Therefore, I would contend that I can be faithful to Jesus' teachings by helping those who are remarrying to be a one-flesh union, a union that has the sharing, committed, intimate, enduring and permanent relationship that God wills. I can offer my knowledge, perspective, and skills to help this marriage be just as strong as it can possibly be.

In essence I can say to the couples who come to me, "Yes, I will assist you in your wedding and in your marriage and family life. But because I am so committed to Jesus' one-flesh vision of marriage, I want to offer you

—time to explore and complete your readiness for remarriage, including your growing confidence that you have really picked the right person with whom to share this remarriage;
—a wedding service designed by the three of us that expresses the new creation that you are;
—counseling to establish workable relationships between stepparents and stepchildren, stepbrothers and stepsisters, and support in dealing with the issues and problems that will naturally and normally evolve; these issues may include "yours-mine-and-ours," financial-management decisions, and conflict and communication management;
—my availability to help you face the problems and celebrate the joys that none of us can anticipate right now.

In short, I offer myself to be with you, now and in the future, to aid you in building a beautiful and enduring marriage and family life together."

To make this kind of offer, clergy and other church leaders will need to become much more knowledgeable about the issues of remarriage. We will attempt to aid you in developing that broader knowledge, both in this book and in *Help for Remarried Couples and Families*[27] (the study book for remarried people to be used in conjunction with this one). We will summarize the available information and literature on this subject and direct you to other resources should you care to dig deeper.

If a church leader seeks to be faithful to the Bible's call for idealism tempered by realism about marriage, then he or she needs to deal with the issue of remarriage in ways other than simply arranging a wedding date. The church needs to do a more systematic job of presenting the one-flesh-marriage concept to the entire congregation. This might include:

—sermons about marriage and family life from the pulpit;
—activities to develop family-building skills in children, youth, young adults, and parents;
—emphasis on personal integrity, wholeness, maturity, whether persons are single or married;
—marriage growth and enrichment opportunities for the married couples of the church;
—strategies to teach church members how to be supportive and helpful when a marriage terminates, whether through death or divorce;
—strategies to teach church members how to be nonjudgmental, sensitive, and supportive to remarriages and remarried persons.

We will speak more of these matters in chapters 6 and 7. We mention these ideas briefly, however, to point out that if we church leaders ask our people to live their married lives in accordance with the Bible's one-flesh-marriage teaching, then we need to do all we can to help them gain the knowledge and skills to accomplish such ideals, although in the final analysis, a one-flesh marriage will always be a gift of grace

This brings us to the second part of Jesus' teaching: the absolute love of God, God's radical acceptance of each of us in our frailty and sin. How do I express this to the couples who come to me seeking remarriage?

To those who come to me with a sense of guilt and failure (which society and the church has undoubtedly reinforced on numerous occasions), I offer forgiveness and redemption. I need not add my voice to those shouting, "Guilty!" I have a more constructive message to share. By my manner with them and sensitivity to them, I communicate acceptance. I explore with the couple what their needs are. If they are in need of explicit exploration of the Bible's themes of redemption, forgiveness, and new possibilities in all areas of life, including marriage, I share such explicit teachings with them.

To those who come to me with a sense of excitement about the new life that is opening up before them, I offer the awareness that God is a God of rebirth, of new creation, of new beginnings. Myrna and Robert Kysar speak powerfully to this point:

> The first task of the church on this score is to present the possibility of remarriage as one symbol of rebirth. It might present remarriage as the second chance for the divorced person. The poignant symbols of death and resurrection are applicable here. The first marriage is dead, and with it have died the hopes and dreams of the individuals involved. But there may be a resurrection. God brings life out of the death of marriage. That life may take the form of remarriage. The church, we are saying, has at its disposal a powerful set of symbols by which to support the divorced person's desire to start again in a marriage relationship. The church can demonstrate that the power of God's grace overcomes the judgment that remarriage after divorce is adultery. It can nurture the belief that whatever sin has occasioned the death of the first marriage and whatever wrong may be found in the difficulties of building a new one, God's promise of grace prevails[28]

In the following chapters we will speak of the "how" of communicating such matters to couples seeking remarriage.

It is hoped that we can begin to gain confidence that this perspective embodies for our day and age obedience to Jesus' intention and to his communication of God's love and grace. We attempt to build enduring marriages in this way, and we offer a contemporary communication of the words Jesus once spoke (and still speaks), "Neither do I condemn you; go, and do not sin again."

2

What Is Readiness
for Remarriage?

Once the church leader agrees that a way to be faithful to Jesus' teaching about the divine intention for marriage is to help persons entering remarriage improve their chances of building a strong, enduring relationship, how does one do that?

The first step, it seems to us, is to encourage people to be ready for remarriage before they enter it. But what is readiness for remarriage? And how does the pastoral counselor recognize it? And how does the church leader encourage it? These are difficult questions. To be frank, we don't know as much about the answers as we would like, but we will share what we know or surmise and then trust that it will sensitize you to pursue this question ever more perceptively. In this book we will draw together insights from a wide variety of sources—studies of sociologists, years of experience in premarital and marital counseling (of both first and subsequent marriages), and our developing knowledge of the unique tasks, issues, and problems of remarriage. We are sure that we offer food for thought; we cannot offer certainty about the ability to diagnose any couple's readiness for remarriage.

What Is Readiness for Remarriage?

To attempt to understand readiness for remarriage, we first need to draw together the accumulated knowledge of sociologists and counselors about readiness for marriage in general. Then we need to ask what part of that information applies to second marriages and what part of it does not. And then we need to ask further, what additional considerations figure in readiness for remarriage.

Insights from Sociology

Sociologist William Stephens wrote an article drawing together data that many research efforts on marital adjustment had discovered in forty years of research. He admits that these are crude, broad findings with an unknown amount of measurement error and that some of them are more firmly substantiated than others. In this article he lists factors that contribute to the success or failure of marriages. He calls these "predictors" and divides his list into three classes: Class A—predictors in which he has the highest confidence; Class B—predictors for which he finds the evidence less persuasive; and Class C—predictors in which he places least confidence. At any rate, we will include his list here.[1]

Class-A Predictors

1. Age at marriage. All studies agree that early-marrying persons have less chance of enduring or happy marriages. "Early" is in the teens or even perhaps in the early twenties. Studies show that, up to the late twenties, the older persons are, the better their chances are for happy and enduring marriages.

2. Length of acquaintanceship and engagement. The longer a couple has known each other and the longer they have had a courting relationship, the better their chances of an enduring marriage. Paul H. Landis underscores this point. He writes: "There is . . . no substitute for an extended period of going steady, followed by an engagement of at least six months, to test compatibility of personality types in real-life situations." He affirms, "Most marriage failures are courtship failures. This point cannot be overstressed."[2]

3. There is little likelihood of marriage success for those couples who marry because of premarital pregnancy.

4. Religiousness. Such items as frequency of worship, participation in religious study groups, identifiable religious preference, and church membership are positively correlated to success in marriage in practically all studies.

5. Similarity of faith. Mixed-faith marriages have higher divorce rates than same-faith marriages.

6. Social class. Don't be poor! Fourteen out of sixteen studies show a positive correlation between social class and marriage adjustment. Too large a class—or income—difference between the two persons is also a negative indicator.

Class-B Predictors

7. Level of education. Two different types of study do not agree here. Those that use divorce as the indicator of failed marriage all agree that the more years of schooling, the lower the divorce rate. Those that use

marital adjustment tests reveal little or no relationship between years of schooling and marital adjustment.

8. Previous divorce. In many studies, previously divorced persons have been shown to have less chance for a successful, enduring marriage. Two studies conclude that previously divorced grooms are a poor risk but previously divorced brides are not.

9. Divorced parents. Children of divorced parents seem to have a tendency to score low on marital-adjustment tests. There seems to be a correlation between the happiness of one's parents' marriage and one's own.

10. Location of residence. Those living in the country or small towns have a better chance of a successful marriage than those living in the city.

11. Parents' approval. Parental approval is a factor that emerges in several studies as one of the factors contributing to marriage adjustment.

12. Sociability. Persons who report that they and/or their marriage partner have many friends, feel popular, and join many groups and organizations tend to score high on these marital-adjustment tests.

Class-C Predictors

13. Differences in age. It appears that one partner being much older or younger than the other may be a negative predictor. Stephens hedges on saying how much is "much older." He suggests perhaps five years or more but says it is hard to say, given the low degree of agreement among the studies.

14. Only children. It appears from some studies that being an only child is a negative predictor.

15. Relationship with parents. Two of the older studies indicate that persons who had much conflict with their parents have low marriage-adjustment scores.

16. The relationship before marriage. If during the engagement period the relationship is strife-ridden and tempestuous, so will the marriage tend to be.

17. Mental health. Three studies reveal a positive correlation between mental health and marital adjustment.

Stephens suggests that any individual item on this list does not mean much by itself but that cumulatively the items do have meaning. If one were to assess his or her chances of building a successful marriage with a given partner and discover one or two items that give a negative indication, this would not be too bad. If one were to find several negative items, however, this might indicate the need for reconsideration and further thought.

I think we have to accept this material for what Stephens says it is—the result of research in a field of study where it is exceedingly difficult to be exact. The usefulness of some of it for those of us who help people prepare for marriage is another matter. There are items on this list over which the potential marriage partner has little control, for example, items 6, 9, and 14. Poor people, people whose parents are divorced, and only children still want to be married—good risks or not. However, this research does give us some basic, raw indicators of a few things to think about when building a relationship that can result in a marriage with a good chance of succeeding.

Insights from Counseling

As a pastoral counselor who has spent time with hundreds of persons planning to be married, I ask some questions about the individuals as well as their relationship as a couple. For the sake of the following discussion, I will continue numbering from Stephens' indicators, with no particular evaluation on the weight of each item.

These are some questions I ask about *each* of the persons wanting to enter this marriage relationship.

18. Does this person have the inner strength and flexibility to be either single or married? On one hand, is she or he incapable of being single and independent, going from one protective situation (parents) to another (spouse)? On the other hand is this person so fiercely independent that commitment, relationship, interdependence is going to hamper his or her style? Or is this person flexible, capable of being single or married?

19. Does this person enter the marriage freely and willingly, not under compulsion from partner, friends, or family and not under the compulsion of being a certain age?

20. To be a bit more specific about one of Stephens' points, is the individual free of mental health difficulties that cripple relationships (such as uncontrollable rage, the need to hurt or be hurt); is the individual free of alcoholism or any other addictions? This is extremely important but difficult for a counselor or even the potential marriage partner to assess. Does the person have leftovers or legacies from his or her family of origin that will intrude into this marriage?

There are also some questions that I ask the couple in order to assess their relationship with each other.

21. Does the couple have the means to supply their economic needs? Have they worked out a financial plan acceptable to both of them for managing their money and giving each other some economic "space"?

22. Do both partners accept the other as he or she is, enjoy the other, and find only a few habits of the other that annoy or antagonize? Have both abandoned any ideas of reforming the other after the wedding?

23. Does the couple face the fact that there is conflict in every couple's life and admit that they have conflict? Have they discovered wholesome ways to deal with and resolve conflict?

24. Is the couple honest with each other about interests, hobbies, pastimes? Have they worked out a life-style acceptable to each, in which the needs and rights of each individual are met, as well as the needs and rights of the couple?

25. Is the couple basically in accord about life's direction, education, family, present gratification versus investments for the future, life's goals, and so on? Have they achieved a mutually agreed upon parenting style?

26. Does each partner have respect for and sensitivity to the other partner's faith, church, values, and commitments? Do they agree about the importance of children's faith experience? Is their faith experience a source of enrichment for their relationship and their world view?

27. Have they worked out an agreement about couple friends, same-sex friends, and opposite-sex friends that is acceptable to each partner? Is there a maximum of trust and a minimum of jealousy between the two?

If those twenty-seven items (whew!) form a fairly reliable guide for readiness for the first marriages, do they apply equally to second or subsequent marriages? Many do indeed apply. As I read down the list, I note some that probably apply less to remarried persons and some that are of particular concern to remarried persons. Let's consider some of the items on the list and ask the question, "Does this item apply to remarried persons?"

Item 1: Age at marriage. Those entering a second marriage will usually be older. There is a Swedish proverb that states: "Being young is a fault which improves daily."[3] A survey some years ago showed the mean ages for men and women at their first marriage to be 24 and 21, respectively; for second marriages the mean ages were 37 and 31, respectively. It is hoped that increased age will contribute some maturity and strength to second marriages.

Item 2: Length of acquaintanceship and engagement. This may well be an important consideration and the source of some remarriage problems. One study revealed that women being remarried had a shorter courtship period before engagement (about a year for remarried persons, a year and a half for women not previously married). Similarly, women who were remarrying were less likely to have a formal engagement period and, if engaged at all, were likely to be engaged for a shorter period before the wedding.[4]

Item 5: Similarity of faith. One might suspect that with increased age and maturity, differences in faith would not be as important. However, Lucile Duberman's study, while it notes some couples who build a life-style that includes the religions of both partners, still notes that 59 percent of the couples who were of the same faith rated their relationship as "excellent," compared with 40 percent of those couples who were of different faiths.[5]

Item 11: Parents' approval. It would seem obvious that parents' approval would be less pressing with the increased age and lessening of dependent ties, but this is apt to be a highly individual item.

Item 13: Differences in age. I would suspect also that differences in age are less important to persons remarrying. It is not a very strongly indicated item on Stephens's list to begin with, and I know a number of couples whose difference in age was greater in their second marriage and whose marriages seem to be quite successful. I did know of one remarried couple who were about fifteen years apart in age; he was in his late forties and she was in her early thirties at the time of their marriage. A few years later, there was a rather drastic change in their social preferences. He preferred a quiet home life, while she wanted to be out with people more often. Interest in and tolerance of children of various ages might be a consideration here also, but I would suspect that second marriages have more flexibility on this point.

In my opinion, all other items on the list apply to second marriages.

Insights from the Nature of Remarriage

In addition to the items just listed, previously married persons need to make other adjustments before they are ready to marry again. Let's look at each of these adjustments in turn. These are complex and important matters and so will need thorough treatment.

A person entering remarriage needs to have resolved his or her former marriage in relationship to the other people directly involved. This will have different ramifications for divorced persons and for widowed persons. The divorced person soon discovers that divorce is a relationship, just as marriage is a relationship. This is particularly true when any children have been born to the marriage and when each parent is to have some responsibility and involvement with the children, whether personal care and contact or financial responsibility or both.

A person has appropriately resolved his or her previous marriage when he or she

—has accepted the death of the marriage relationship and the reality of the divorce;

—has made decisions about the divorce settlement and the children that both former spouses can live with, with a minimum of continuing bitterness;

—has put into practice these decisions, such as financial payments, visitation, custody, holidays, and so on, and the arrangements are working;

—has learned not to be "hooked" by the former spouse's behavior. In some cases the previous two items cannot be true; one can only be responsible for one's own behavior. Therefore, the person must not "give in" to his or her spouse's behavior or manipulation.

I once knew a couple who had many traits that annoyed each other, but their major difference was in their attitudes about time. Punctuality was very important for one, not at all important for the other. Being late was a constant source of friction. They separated and ultimately divorced. In the early days of their separation, every time custody of the children changed from one to the other, the old punctuality fight surfaced again. One partner chose to torture the other by never being on time, and the other partner chose to be irritated and annoyed every time it happened. They experienced all the annoyances of being married without any of the satisfactions. This created a constant turmoil in both partners which would have invaded any other marriage relationship.

A divorced person's readiness for remarriage involves either reaching an adequate divorce settlement (in every sense of the word) with the former spouse or achieving enough emotional distance so that the turmoil from the former spouse does not overly influence the person. This is always relative, of course. As long as children grow, change, and have different needs and problems, decisions have a way of coming undone and needing reconsideration. As much as possible, the resolution of the former marriage needs to be achieved, even if new issues need to be faced from time to time.

For the widowed person, resolving the former marriage has other aspects:

—disposing of the dead spouse's clothing and other objects that uniquely belonged to that person;

—making appropriate decisions about photos, scrapbooks, and other momentos of one's life with the deceased spouse so that a delicate balance is achieved, in which the former spouse is not forgotten but also is not too prominent a memory in the present relationship;

—perhaps even making a decision about a home, especially if one home is so intimately connected with the memory, the style, and the tastes of a former spouse that any new occupant would feel like an intruder, or that the widowed person would see any newcomer as an intruder;

—developing a new relationship with the dead spouse's family which assures that the deceased person is not forgotten and that the in-law relationships will remain cherished, but which also establishes enough emotional distance that the remaining spouse is ready to enter a new relationship;

—working out, with the knowledge of all involved, the financial and material decisions that may touch the children of the former marriage. (We will discuss this later.)

And so, whatever one's former circumstance, part of readiness for remarriage is to deal as thoroughly as possible with all of the circumstances resulting from one's previous marriage so that they do not drain energy from the new relationship.

A person entering remarriage needs to have resolved the former marriage within himself or herself. This is to say that one has lived through the grief, the anger, the blows to one's self-esteem, and the distrust of others that comes with divorce. One has moved on to becoming a self-sufficient, whole, trusting human being, ready to enter into a relationship with another whole human being.

Bruce Fisher, who has carefully researched this need and has built a method to help people achieve just such wholeness, offers a word of advice to persons who have recently ended a love relationship—a word of advice about which he feels so strongly that he puts it in capital letters: "I SUGGEST YOU DO NOT BECOME INVOLVED IN ANOTHER LONG-TERM EMOTIONALLY COMMITTED RELATIONSHIP UNTIL YOU HAVE EMOTIONALLY WORKED THROUGH THE ENDING OF THE PAST LOVE RELATIONSHIP."[6]

He suggests a series of fifteen building blocks that represent steps which one needs to take, aided by self-examination, good personal support, and the passage of time, in order to be ready to enter a whole relationship. He illustrates these blocks with the following diagram.[7]

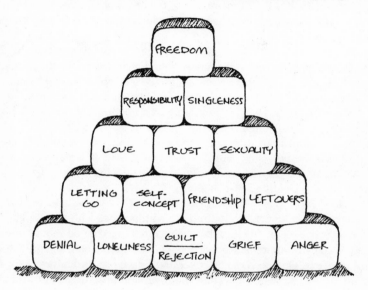

We cannot do justice to his whole system in a brief summary, but we shall attempt to introduce it as a backdrop against which to assess readiness or lack of readiness for remarriage. Fisher describes the following fifteen steps, stages, or issues on the way to divorce recovery and wholeness:

a. Denial. Divorce may come as a shock to some. Therefore, it may be exceedingly difficult to admit to oneself or to others. The first step— so simple to state, so difficult to do—is to *admit*, "I am experiencing a divorce."

b. Loneliness. Being without the one selected for a life partner may lead to the greatest sense of loneliness one will ever experience. Even the presence of one's children and the warm, caring feelings of other people does not cause the emptiness to go away.

c. Rejection/guilt. If one is the "dumper" (the one who chooses to leave), there may be considerable guilt for hurting the former marriage partner. If one is the "dumpee" (the one left), the predominant emotion may be that of rejection.

d. Grief. Though many do not realize it, divorce is a grief experience. One mourns the death of a relationship, the death of an ideal or dream, the loss of companionship of someone who once was very important to him or her.

e. Anger. At about this point in the divorce recovery process, there may occur a rage, an anger, the intensity of which may shock the person who experiences it. But this is intimately connected to the next step.

f. Letting go of the "emotional corpse" (the dead relationship). One recognizes the fruitlessness of investing in a relationship that holds no promise and begins to put more energy into personal growth.

g. Self-esteem. Immediately following a divorce, the person is likely to have an extremely low sense of self-worth. But as the person progresses, he or she may be ready to invest considerable time and energy in rebuilding a positive self-concept.

h. Friendships. One's friendships may need to be restructured. Perhaps one will no longer be comfortable with persons who were friends of the former couple. Social relationships may need to be rebuilt with friends who can comprehend or accept one's emotional pain and growth.

i. Leftovers. One needs to discover and face those difficulties, hang-ups, or neuroses, which one has "leftover" from childhood, youth, and the previous love relationship. If one does not deal with these, one is apt to find oneself making the same mistakes in starting new relationships and responding within them the next time around.

j. Love. Though one may leave a marriage feeling unlovable and confused about love, a sign of healing is the recovery (or discovery) of a healthy self-love and a confidence that one can love others as well.

k. Trust. From the pain of ending a love relationship, the person has what Fisher calls a "love wound," a hurt so great that trusting anyone— certainly anyone of the opposite sex—is very difficult. The healing process takes a good deal of time, but eventually one takes small steps toward risking emotional closeness again.

l. Sexuality. Though one's previous sexual partner is gone, sexual needs go on. One's sexual needs may go through three stages: lack of interest in sex, a stage of obsession with sex, and then a time of normal sex drive.

m. Responsibility. From the crisis of an ended love, one may be able to learn responsibility. Perhaps the previous love relationship was an underresponsible or overresponsible relationship. One can learn how to begin to build a relationship of two people who are responsible for themselves but are willing and able to make promises and care for another person.

n. Singleness. The experience of singleness—growth of the ability to be an independent person—is an important and essential step in personal growth. If one is aware that he or she can survive and even be happy as a single, then all decisions about future relationships can be healthy decisions made from strength.

o. Freedom. One becomes free to choose singleness or another relationship. "Shall I pursue this relationship or not? Shall I say yes or no to this opportunity?" One senses freedom to make choices for reasons from inside oneself. One is also free to be oneself, not shackled by unrecognized needs or by the compulsion to please everyone else.[8]

Fisher recognizes that one may not deal with these building blocks in the order he lists them; indeed, people are more or less working on all of them all of the time. He knows also that a setback, such as the end of another intimate relationship or a court litigation, may force one to rework one's way over some of the same blocks.[9]

Fisher's research, and the experience of many in the divorce recovery groups he has led, reveal that this process is a reliable building plan for inner wholeness and thus inner readiness for remarriage.

The widowed person's experience would have some similarities and some differences to the process just described. The widowed person probably receives more support at the time of loss, for the loss by death is more clearly recognized as a grief experience, to which persons in our society know how to respond. Becoming a widow may not be as big a shock to one's self-concept as becoming a divorced person. One may not struggle as much with the trust issue after the experience of widowhood. The guilt/rejection pains may not be as great.

Still one needs to experience a period of deep and extended grief and needs to let go of his or her previous partner before being ready to enter into a whole new relationship. Neil Simon's play and movie *Chapter Two* makes this point eloquently. The widowed George enters into a witty and lively relationship with Jenny, whom he shortly marries; he takes her to—of all places—the same place where he honeymooned with his first wife. When someone expresses condolences about his first wife's death, he becomes depressed and morose, immediately returning home. As his new wife attempts to probe into what is the matter, he finally bursts out that he's depressed because he still misses his first wife, and he can't admit it.[10] The grief was unfinished. He was not ready to enter wholeheartedly into a new relationship. This unresolved grief intruded and invaded the fledgling partnership with his new wife.

Persons married to widows or widowers, particularly those who may have married too soon, tell me that Simon touched a vital point. They speak of competing with a ghost in the marriage. Sometimes they wonder about these faultless, sainted people who have been described in such glowing terms.

To summarize then, the widow(er) needs to work through grief to the extent that she or he

—no longer has the compulsive need to speak for long periods of time about the dead spouse;
—has granted the dead spouse his or her place in history as neither saint nor devil but as a person with worth and dignity;
—can be sensitive to a new love partner's tolerance for hearing about the former marriage partner;
—senses that out of inner strength she or he is ready to enter into a new, committed love relationship.

Both the widowed and the divorced need to have resolved their former marriages within themselves in order to be ready for a new marriage.

The next two adjustments are closely related. Let us consider them together:

A person entering remarriage needs to accept the future spouse's previous marriage as a historical reality with continuing consequences; and *a person entering remarriage needs to be compatible not only with his or her new partner but with that partner's life situation.*

Two people, both middle agers who cared about each other, were attempting to make decisions about their relationship. "What do you want of me?" she asked. He responded, "I want to be twenty-one and the only man you ever loved." That's an understandable wish (an unspoken wish in many seeking remarriage) but one that is impossible for most persons, especially persons entering remarriage.

A person who has been previously married in all likelihood carries some personal ties, obligations, and commitments from that previous marriage. This life situation may have to do with persons and families to whom one has responsibilities. For example:

—She is a person on whom many people have a claim. She senses her former in-laws' need to keep in contact, and so she does so. Her former husband has remarried a woman with children, and so there are many persons involved in her decisions about her time.

Or one's situation may include financial-economic obligations. For example:

—She is a person who was thrust into low-paying work by her divorce. She has many debts and financial commitments.

—He is a person who has substantial financial obligations for child support and his children's educations over the coming years.

Part of one's situation has to do with one's emotional state. For example:

—She is a single parent who has really tried to compensate for the emotional upset the divorce has been for her kids by investing herself completely in parenting. She's apt to put her kids first and is equally apt not to let anyone into a parenting partnership very easily.

—He is a person still very much in conflict with his former spouse. Every time he has to deal with her, he becomes upset and depressed.

None of these are impossible life situations. They are all quite understandable, quite typical, and for the most part, quite normal. However, persons entering remarriage may be so excited about the compatibility they feel with another person that they, for a time, ignore the question "Are our life situations also compatible?" That question will intrude itself sooner or later. Anticipating and dealing with this question before the couple is married may contribute to the strength of their marriage. Some persons may find it a frightening experience to ask, "Are we compatible in both personal and life-situation issues?" The able counselor, however, can help them to face those fears and raise those all-important basic issues.

A person entering remarriage needs to have experienced "realized forgiveness."

Some may dismiss this point rather quickly, suggesting that in the present day, widespread acceptance of divorce and remarriage has made this need obsolete. However, one needs only talk with divorced and remarrying people to discover that this point is far from obsolete. Guilt is a multi-dimensional experience. It operates on many levels of understanding.

Bruce Fisher tells of speaking to high school groups and asking them, "How many expect to be married?" Most hands will go up. He then asks, "How many expect to be divorced?" Usually no hands go up. No one enters a marriage expecting to fail. And no one likes to fail at anything, even for reasons beyond their control.

And so the guilt-rejection sense of failure that the divorced person carries may include these feelings:

—I couldn't live up to my personal goals and ideals;
—I didn't live up to what my family taught me;
—I hurt and/or couldn't hold the love commitment of a person once important to me;
—I did not conform to the teachings of my church;
—I did not live up to God's will for me.

Any or all of these are a heavy load to carry! Persons of a wide range of backgrounds and theologies experience this guilt. I remember visiting with an older woman who believed in a very conservative, literalist interpretation of the Bible. She had been divorced and remarried and felt a strong sense of guilt. She remembered years of wavering between delight in the love of her husband and guilt at marrying him. Over and over she would tell him, "I love you, honey, but I never should have married you." Eventually it occurred to her that anything so good must be from the blessing of God, and her guilt slowly abated.

But on the other end of the theological spectrum, a woman who was uncertain about her belief in God discussed her coming remarriage with me in the following way: "I must confess that I feel strange, uneasy about this marriage. Although I really enjoy Glenn and look forward to being married to him, I never thought I'd be doing this. Somehow before I go ahead with this, I need to feel that this is an OK thing to do. If there is a God, I'd like to feel right with God in this important step, also."

James Emerson, who in his book *Divorce, the Church, and Remarriage* offers us the concept of "realized forgiveness," points out that unless one has a sense of the reality of forgiveness so that he or she is able to say, "I feel like a new person," remarriage is difficult and tainted. Emerson defines "realized forgiveness" as "the awareness of forgiveness to such a degree that a person is free from the guilt he [or she] feels." Such forgiveness must be experienced if anyone is to be ready for remarriage.[11]

Emerson notes that for this to happen, there has to be awareness both of guilt and of forgiveness. The guilt may be buried and hidden from oneself. A counseling relationship that is accepting and probing may make one aware of guilt and forgiveness at one and the same time. He quotes the person who said to his minister, "'It suddenly struck me, as I was feeling terrible about what I had done, that if you could still accept me, why so could I.' ''[12]

On whatever levels one feels guilt, there is the need to realize a forgiveness powerful enough to free one to start again. This is a bedrock need for readiness for remarriage.

How Does the Pastoral Counselor Recognize Readiness (or Unreadiness) for Remarriage?

How does the pastoral counselor recognize, and help the couple who comes to him seeking remarriage to recognize, readiness or lack of readiness for remarriage? Perhaps we can best begin to explore this topic by dealing with two misunderstandings that counselors and couples may have about readiness for remarriage.

The first misunderstanding is that persons show that they have recovered from their divorce or their spouse's death by making the decision to remarry. This is not necessarily true at all. Mel Krantzler says that some people remarry prematurely because of all the "poisonous needs" that they feel in the early months/years following their divorces. A person feels this need to remarry to compensate for feelings of worthlessness, "for the sake of the children," to gain economic security, to find an end to loneliness, or from hunger for regular decent home cooking.[13] Krantzler points out that one can easily confuse "desperation" and "love" at this point. Urgently felt needs may propel one prematurely into a marriage for which one is not ready, and almost certainly a troubled relationship will follow.

A piece of research by S. Soul[14] using the Fisher Divorce Adjustment Scale has revealed that many persons entering remarriage have not adjusted to their previous divorce.

The decision to remarry does not necessarily indicate adjustment and readiness. In all fairness to the persons considering this marriage union, the question of readiness should be explored thoroughly.

The second misunderstanding is the assumption that if the couple has been living together, they have sufficient knowledge about what remarriage will be like and do not need counseling on readiness for remarriage. This is only partially true at best. The couple who has lived together for a time has a clearer understanding of each other's day-to-day characteristics, but there may be many ways in which they are not automatically ready for marriage.

Some persons see living together and marriage as quite different entities. Either or both partners might slip into quite different roles and role expectations after the wedding. Some good premarriage counseling questions to ask might be "In what ways do you anticipate that your relationship will change after the wedding? What is your concept of marriage? How do you feel about marriage?"

Some persons suppress important parts of their personality throughout even an extended living-together arrangement. Krantzler tells of a man, an avid sports lover, who met on the tennis court the person who became his live-in partner. Throughout their living-together arrangement she seemed to enjoy all the sports he did. As soon as they married, she said that she had just been participating in the sports to please him and withdrew into a more homebound, typical-housewife life-style, resulting shortly in a separation. Another set of good premarriage counseling questions might include these: "Are there important things about your personality, your interests, or your needs that you haven't been expressing during your living together? Are there things that you hope will be reduced in or eliminated from your relationship or added to your relationship after you are married? Are you hoping for more time for yourself alone? More time for your relationship? What will you need in your marriage for you to be truly *you* and for your relationship to be a creative commitment?"

Some couples have lived together successfully in some dimensions but have ignored others—perhaps money management, or religious involvement, or opposite-sex friendships, or the handling of conflicts between the partners. Still other good premarriage counseling questions might be "What unfinished agenda do you have in building your marriage relationship? What other issues do you feel that you need to face?"

Living together by no means guarantees that the couple has developed an open, honest life-style on which an enduring commitment can be made. The couple should be asked to evaluate and learn from their experience to date: "What have you discovered about building a successful relationship? What are the strengths that you have developed as a couple? What are your hopes, your aspirations, for the years ahead now that you have come to me to consider marriage?"

This discussion leads to a parallel concern for the minister to whom the couple comes to be married. Since ministers are moral-religious leaders as well as counselors helping persons get ready for weddings, a problem occurs. How should the minister respond to the information that the couple is living together before marriage? I believe the minister should respond objectively and nonjudgmentally, using the couple's experience of living together as part of the learning through which they and the minister explore how to build a good marriage. I do not say this casually. I was once a part of a clergy association in which a religious leader pled with us clergy not to officiate at the wedding of any couple who had been living together unless the couple repented. I listened to this leader's impassioned plea but decided to be among those who did not conform to his view of ministerial moral responsibility.

There are at least three reasons why I choose my accepting, nonjudgmental approach to persons in a living-together arrangement. In the first place, the couple comes to me, not asking about living together, but about moving beyond this relationship into marriage. I choose to share their focus on the future. They have discovered that living together is a temporary relationship and that they seek a deeper commitment, which I affirm and support.

In the second place, persons living together represent a large part of the population. A recent census bureau report shows that the number of persons living together has more than doubled in the last decade. They note that one and a half million unmarried women and men acknowledge living together, and virtually all observers say that this is a gross underestimate, for many are doing so quietly without admitting it publicly to the census bureau. To be sure, a Christian moral leader should not endorse any movement simply because it is popular. On the other hand, one should not cut oneself off from a large population that is looking to move into the commitment of marriage, seeking the blessing of God and church.

The third reason for my choice of approach is that it is quite possible that "living together" is a coming institution in the process of being formed. I have already noted that remarried persons often have shorter engagements or no formal engagement at all. And yet the engagement period of times past fulfilled an important function. It provided the time and opportunity for a couple to move from simple romantic attraction to readiness for marriage. It was a time of testing. It appears to me that many persons are seeking living together as an alternative means to achieve that readiness or to discover that marriage will never happen with this partner, and perhaps not at all. This is how Mel Krantzler views living together. However, he feels that it clearly should be an intentional step by persons who sense a potential relationship to be deepened. It should not simply be a "drifting" process. He suggests that living together can be a "morally based learning experience if you are ready to use it as such."[15]

He recalls his own experience in living with the woman, named Pat, who was to become his wife. He writes: "We subsequently found that our living-together arrangement was an intermediate stage in our learning to love again. It proved to be a bridge between the selective-distancing stage, which Pat and I were in at the time we decided to live together, and the creative-commitment stage of our marriage one year later."[16]

At the heart of the issue, of course, is the teaching of Bible and church about sexual morality. I cannot deny that living together before marriage flies in the face of traditional understandings of biblical teachings, and that makes me uncomfortable. Still, of all the sexual options being exercised in the world today, I have to think that sexual expression within a committed, monogamous relationship—which has existed for most of the couples living together with whom I have counseled before their marriages—is among the best and most moral of the options.

With this, I end the parenthesis about living-together arrangements and return to the main question of this section: how does one recognize readiness for marriage in remarrying persons? Having listed the items of readiness for remarriage, there is little we can add for the pre-remarriage counselor. She or he will need to utilize the information in her or his own style with each couple who present themselves for remarriage.

Tests are available that can aid this process. There is a test to measure how completely one has recovered from a previous divorce.[17] There are tests that give a rough prediction of compatibility,[18] though none of these are geared specifically to the remarrying couple.

I sense that remarrying couples want a premarriage counseling process that fits them and their needs, that raises the significant questions in ways fitting to them and at a speed appropriate to their readiness to face the questions. Remarrying couples have told me of terminating their relationship with pastors who used "canned" tapes that were primarily geared to persons entering a first marriage, which they sensed did not fit their needs at all. They wanted help, but competent and personal help that related to who they were and where they found themselves in their unique relationship.

Before leaving this topic, I should mention just one other indicator that some people use in assessing readiness for remarriage—time. Bruce Fisher suggests that it takes some people three to five years to get past the really negative stuff in divorce recovery.[19] And so some see the passage of a fair amount of time as one of the essentials before one is ready for remarriage. This is a helpful but uncertain clue. Some persons may have started disengaging from their partner long before the official divorce. Others may enter promptly and deeply into therapy and/or sharing with support people, while others may not. Some may plunge into the pain and learning, while others may deny for a long time before they begin. And some people never seem to learn. Ten years after their divorce or their spouse's death, they are not prepared to enter a new relationship. But still, time is a clue. The precipitous leap into another marriage immediately after the old one ends certainly deserves examination in the counseling room.

If the counselor has become familiar with enough literature about remarriage to realize that remarriage is continuous-but-discontinuous with first marriage and that the stepfamily is continuous-but-discontinuous with the intact family, and if the counselor has built his or her own list of items of readiness for remarriage, then he or she will be ready to explore this topic with those who come seeking help to take this step.

What Can the Church Leader Do to Contribute to a Couple's Readiness for Remarriage?

Church leaders have the privilege of ministering to persons of all ages. The church not only will be present when the two people present themselves for remarriage but will have been present in the past, when the death or divorce occurred, and will be present in the future as the partners establish their new marriage and family. This is an important truth, for if the church leader is going to contribute to readiness for remarriage (not simply recognize its presence or absence), the church will need to be present at other times in the person's life. However, let's take a look at the items that relate specifically to remarriage and ask what the church leader can do to contribute.

To help a person resolve his or her former marriage, both in relationship to others and in relationship to oneself, the pastor or church leader can do the following things.

The minister can counsel with the couple who is divorcing, to help them seek a fair divorce settlement with which they both can live. In this process, there will be difference of opinion, conflict, and anger. It will be difficult, but the persons involved should not be vindictive, an attitude which can lead to continuing bitterness. There are legitimate differences of opinion, both between the two divorcing persons and between the couple and the court, as to what is just. Divorcing individuals may feel a sense of rage as the disposition of their relationship, their resources, their children, goes out of their control to outsiders—the judge and the court system.

In the midst of this adversary system, there needs to be a mediator, one who cares about both parties, one who neither feeds or encourages the anger nor denies it, one who reminds both parties from time to time, "Remember, divorce is a relationship, just like marriage is a relationship. If there are children, you are going to be dealing with this person for a long time. Make a settlement you and your former spouse can live with." In such a process it is important to know what is going on with the divorcing partners, their attorneys, and the courts. Without such awareness the minister may be involved in work that appears to be "divorce mediation" but is not legally satisfying or appropriate and thus will have to be redone. Still there is a moral as well as legal counsel that is needed at such times. There are successful divorces (strange as the terms sounds to our ears) and there are unsuccessful divorces. I am convinced that one mark of a successful divorce is the ability to resolve one's relationship with a former spouse. Indeed, studies show that the positive attitude of one's former spouse to one's new marriage is a contributing factor to that marriage's success.

In some cases, the minister can offer the divorcing couple a divorce ceremony. Two people once cared for each other, and now their relationship is dead. It deserves a dignified burial.

When one of the coauthors of this book, who is a divorced-remarried person, had her final divorce pronouncement, she was appalled at the lack of respect of the court. This "routine" matter was quickly processed, granted, and not even a gavel sounded. It seemed to her that the termination of two people's investment in each other's lives needed more attention and dignity than it was given there. "Is that it?" she asked her attorney. "What did you expect, bells to ring?" he responded. In a state of shock, she walked across the street from the courthouse to her church and visited a few minutes quietly with her pastor. Had both partners looked to the same pastor, it would have been fitting for both to come to their pastor. Perhaps with just the three of them, there could have been a brief prayer asking God to enable them to remember the good times, to let go with dignity, and to care successfully for their children over the years ahead.

Sometimes ritual acts play a significant part in helping persons live out the changes of their life before God. A ritual at this point may contribute to the healing of two persons who both have personal hurts and have experienced relational tensions with which they need to deal at this time.

When a person is widowed, the church leader can offer his or her support and direct the person to others who have shared the same experience. The church leader can either offer a church-sponsored support group for the widowed or direct the person to other available groups in the community. The church leader should stand ready to provide grief counseling so that the widowed person can feel permission to feel the loss of the deceased spouse, grant that person a place in history, and be ready (in time) to move on to other life experiences.

When a person is divorced, one can likewise offer personal support and can direct the person to other previously divorced persons. The church leader can also offer the person good literature about divorce recovery and either offer divorce-recovery groups through the church or direct the person to such a group in the community. In the final chapter of this book we will provide several significant resources to help in this process.

The experiences of many people make clear that a thoroughgoing process of counseling, support, and self-growth during and following the death of a spouse or divorce can contribute to the person's freedom to enter more freely into new relationships.

The counseling church leader can help a person entering remarriage accept the fact of the spouse's previous marriage as a historical fact with continuing consequences and help the person achieve a compatibility not only with the marriage partner but with that partner's life situation. Making this process visible is an important step in dealing with the powerful forces in a marriage, and so the church leader might stimulate thought and reflection by asking some hard questions.

—Are you a jealous person? Can you accept the fact that your partner had a previous love relationship or relationships?

—What would you do if you were in the community where your spouse's former in-laws live and she or he wanted to go see them? Would you forbid it? Would you allow it but go somewhere else? Or would you go along?

—What would you do if you were to be honored at an important banquet but at the last minute your spouse refused to come because of worry about an ill (but not seriously ill) child by his or her previous marriage?

The counselor can perhaps help the individuals to face the question

"Am I committed enough to this partner that I am willing to make adjustments to his or her entire life situation?"

The minister and church can offer the couple "realized forgiveness." James Emerson, who suggested this concept to us, contends that a meaningful marriage needs both "the realization of forgiveness . . . and an adequate means of expressing this forgiveness."[20] He suggests further that the following six conditions are necessary for the communication of realized forgiveness.

1. *"Realized forgiveness means that all three parties* (that is, the couple, the minister, and the church) *are under judgment and need forgiveness!"*[21] The church, church law, and minister all form part of the culture in which relationships have a difficult time enduring. Neither church nor minister can say that all has been done to encourage and secure stronger marriages, so all are indeed under judgment and need forgiveness.

2. *"In practice, realized forgiveness means that the minister and church officer must center on the people involved as they are."*[22] In other words, it is an expression of forgiveness-acceptance for the minister and the church to respond to the couple as they are—persons seeking remarriage—and to respond to them in terms of their needs rather than in terms of church law or self-interest.

3. *"In practice, realized forgiveness means that the minister and the church officers must have real communication with the couple involved."*[23] This means face to face conversation in which all parties speak, listen, and hear. If a minister is to be a means by which a couple become aware of realized forgiveness, there must be rapport and acceptance between minister and couple.

4. *"In practice, realized forgiveness also means that the couple must have a sense of personal self-awareness."*[24] For each individual this involves an awareness of his or her problems and disappointments as well as the forgiveness available. When a person examines his or her guilt and the fact that someone loves him or her, there comes a time when he or she can finally accept the reality of both. There must be awareness both of one's problem *and* one's forgiveness.[25].

5. *"Realized forgiveness, in practice, means not only an experience of personal self-awareness, but also of cultural self-awareness."*[26] Both minister and couple must be aware of the mixed signals that their culture—including state laws, church laws, customs, and practices—is sending them. They must recognize that they are persons in the midst of brokenness and confusion.

6. For realized forgiveness there must be faith on the parts of all involved that a real revelation has taken place. When this happens, one is able to experience a sense of integrity in regard to one's past, one's present, one's culture, and God.

Emerson points out further that realized forgiveness requires of the *couple* the courage to believe they are actually forgiven (in spite of any doubts they may have). It requires of them, also, the courage to commit themselves to each other.

The reality of forgiveness requires of the *minister* a similar courage, the courage to believe that the revelation of forgiveness and of readiness for marriage are real. It also demands of the pastor the courage to commit himself or herself to this marriage even in the face of unfavorable statistics about remarriages, past failures, or present inadequacies.

The reality of forgiveness requires of the *church* the courage to accept this couple as one flesh, participation in the wedding (both through formal authorizing procedures and informal supportive presence), and acceptance of the remarried couple into the life of the congregation.[27]

And so the minister and the church offer the couple realized forgiveness

—through acceptance, rapport, and communication during the premarriage counseling process;

—by inquiry and probing into their conscious feelings of guilt and need of forgiveness;

—by assuring them of the reality of forgiveness;

—by presence and involvement in their plans and wedding;

—by avoiding any legalisms that express a punitive attitude or second-class-citizen status to them;

—by the symbols, expressions, words of forgiveness, and celebration of new life in the wedding itself. (We will speak more of this in the next chapter.)

Readiness for remarriage is a delicate and complex subject. It is hoped that in the maze of discoveries we have shared here, you will find a few resources to aid you in launching persons into more effective remarriages through greater readiness.

3

Planning the Wedding with Remarried People

As the pastoral counselor works with the couple anticipating remarriage, the counselor not only has the task of helping them assess their readiness for remarriage and the appropriateness of their choice of each other but also has the opportunity to plan the wedding with the couple. There is the hope that this wedding service will celebrate the love and commitment of two people for each other and contribute to the strength of their marriage bond.

Like so many other things about remarriage, planning the wedding is a task that is both familiar and strange. In many ways a remarriage wedding is similar to a first wedding, but there are differences to be recognized and acted upon as well.

Let's first think about the similarities of all wedding services; then let's look at what is known about the differences in remarriage weddings; and then let's explore how we as church persons can contribute to the couple's life through our assistance and participation in remarriage services.

The Similarities in First and Second Marriages

Brill, Halpin, and Genne, noted authorities on weddings, suggest, "The essence of the wedding ceremony is a freely given, publicly proclaimed consent and commitment made before God and man."[1] They note that there are three basic elements in all wedding services, whether Jewish, Catholic, or Protestant.

First, "the essential heart of the wedding is the vow or covenant (much deeper than a contract) the partners make to each other pledging to do everything in their power to help each other achieve the fullest development possible (despite all obstacles) forever!"[2] This is a very personal statement of two people, each to the other, a crystallizing formulation of promises made and dreams shared in all the months leading up to the wedding.

Second, a wedding is a community event. The couple's family, friends, and associates gather to witness their public vows, to support them as they begin their married life together, and to celebrate and rejoice with them over this significant step in their lives. Persons from other parts of the world tell me that in their homelands a wedding is an event to which the whole village is invited. In our culture the community is more often an intentional, invited community. The community at a wedding is one in which even though some people may not know each other, all share friendship for at least one partner of the wedding couple and all share love and good wishes for the couple's success.

Third, a wedding is a time for the couple to recognize the sacred and eternal significance of the vows (covenant) they make and the marriage and family they hope to build.

> When a couple make their vows and their prayers to God they are saying to themselves and to all who witness that their love is more than human. They acknowledge that the source of their love is in God and the course of their love is to fulfill God's loving will for their lives and that the goal of their love is to grow in love. By acknowledging the Divine source and power of their love their whole relationship takes on cosmic significance. The power of the universe flows through them not only to enrich each other but to enrich and inspire all who know them.[3]

We have described three basic elements of a wedding, but perhaps there are two others that should be mentioned.

Fourth, a wedding is an art form. Brill, Halpin, and Genne, who suggest the term, offer this suggestion: "As with any other art form, the wedding will often attain most beauty and power through simplicity and sincerity."[4] The term "art form" raised to my consciousness a factor important to most weddings. Most people who have planned a wedding want it to be beautiful! They want it to have unity, integrity, and consistency; they want it to be bound together in loveliness.

The unifying element for a wedding that achieves the potential of being breathlessly beautiful is the uniqueness of the couple who make their vows before God and community. When the pastor, the couple, and the couple's families enter into dialogue, plan carefully, show sensitivity to all preferences but make choices intentionally and firmly, and do their parts well, then the wedding may be an artistic experience, enhancing the worship experience, enhancing the community experience, and enhancing the couple's very personal love for each other. The vows of covenanting by two people deserve nothing less.

The fifth element is that a wedding is a cultural and family expression. This may be either unconscious or conscious. Whether the couple knows it or not, if they assume that

—the bride will wear white,

—she will have a diamond engagement ring and a plain wedding band,

—the couple will process in to Mendelssohn and process out to Wagner's wedding march from *Lohengrin* (the "traditional" wedding marches),

then they are expressing cultural assumptions about their wedding.

I became aware of this some years ago when a young couple of Mexican-American heritage came to me and requested a Protestant version of the traditional Mexican wedding. Because of my cultural past, I did not understand some of the things they were saying until I went to a priest friend who worked with the Latin-American population in my community. At his invitation I attended a Mexican wedding. There I realized the significance of some of the symbols important to the couple: the "lasso" (not the rope a cowboy uses, as I had imagined, but a rosary with particularly large loops of beads), which was wrapped around the couple during the wedding prayer, "that they may be bound together in Christ"; the chest with ten dimes, which was a reminder of the old dowry and also an expression of the hope "that they never be poor"; and the gifts and contributions from each of the many wedding participants. I sensed how right it was that their marriage have the cultural continuity expressed within the worship of their church.

Probably these cultural and family expectations come to the fore when we discover what we *assume* will be part of the wedding and wedding reception celebrations. Wise wedding planners will make sure that assumptions of the prospective bride and groom and of their families are verbalized and either combined or negotiated. I recently went through this process in my own family when family and individual hopes and preferences all came to bear on planning a wedding and a wedding celebration. Some of the dialogue went something like this:

"In my tradition we always celebrate a wedding with a dance."

"We'll have to take some dancing lessons, but all right."

"Also, we have a kegger (keg of beer) and a toast at weddings."

"It's not my life-style to serve liquor. If you want to, OK, but if you choose to do that, please be sure also to provide a nonalcoholic beverage for those who do not drink alcohol.''

"OK. In our tradition we usually serve an informal meal to the wedding guests, in addition to having the dance and keg.''

"Well, if we are going to do that, I want to use china and linen tablecloths, not paper plates and picnic tables!!''

"That will cost more. If you want to help pay for it, OK.''

"OK.''

There were many other items on which to decide but adequate discussion, planning, compromise, and agreement led to a day that was a worship experience, a celebration, an art form, and a family-cultural expression of two families coming together.

Couples do well to ask, "Is there anything out of my heritage that I want to include in the wedding service and in the celebrations surrounding our wedding?'' Some find beautiful ways to express this family continuity.

—At the rehearsal dinner both families shared "family stories,'' amusing stories about the bride and groom in their younger days, and other family memories as well.

—In a wedding worship bulletin, the bride's parents included a special message. It was the same message that the bride's grandfather had sent to her mother and father on their wedding day.

—In another wedding the couple chose as one of the solos a song that had been sung at the groom's parents' wedding a generation before.

A couple does not marry in isolation. They marry as part of a culture and a family, and they may want to discover ways to express this truth.

So we see that every wedding is (a) a personal statement of love and commitment, (b) a community event, (c) a worshipful affirmation of divine empowerment to love, (d) an art form and (e) a cultural family expression. All this is true whether the wedding is a first marriage or a remarriage.

The Differences in a Remarriage Wedding

Persons who have experienced a second wedding often express the fact that there is a different dynamic at the wedding. When pressed as to what the dynamic is, they find it hard to pinpoint. Nevertheless we must try to do so if we are to be of utmost help in aiding people plan such weddings.

We can begin by noting some external differences. A rather old study by A. B. Hollingshead examined a number of behavioral traits associated with weddings and compared these traits by previous marital pattern. He had four categories, (a) neither previously married; (b) woman previously married, man single; (c) woman single, man previously married; (d) both previously married. We, however, will compare just two of these and report some of his findings.[5]

	Neither previously married	Woman previously married, man single
Percentage with formal wedding	69.7	4.8
Percentage with church wedding	81.3	22.6
Number in bridal party (including bride and groom)	7.2	4.1
Number of wedding guests	172	34
Percentage of cases in which bride's family paid for wedding	45.7	14.8

In other words, Hollingshead said that in second marriages the weddings were apt to be less formal, were less likely to be church weddings, and were likely to have fewer guests and fewer persons in the wedding party than in first marriages. The couple themselves were much more likely to pay for the wedding and reception. Though this study is thirty years old, these conclusions almost certainly still apply, at least from my experience and observation.

Such differences remind us that remarriage weddings are not considered "once in a lifetime" events as first weddings are. There is a less drastic change in status in second marriages. There is a residue of grief (however slight) about the failure of the first marriage. There is less community investment than there is in launching a brand new young couple. Instead, there are the hopes of friends that the two people involved are putting their lives back together in a constructive way. Remarriage weddings may well be joyous and celebrative, but they are different.

Second marriages are usually between older persons with previously formed families to consider. Remarriage ceremonies need to include ways to recognize these families and help all to be involved in the change that is occurring.

There are, to our knowledge, at least two books of etiquette for second and subsequent weddings. One is entitled *Getting Married Again*, by Susan Fields.[6] The other is entitled *The New Etiquette Guide to Getting Married Again*, by Marjabelle Young Stewart.[7] In the preface of the latter book, Stewart points to some of the issues inherent in planning a second marriage.

> Getting married again . . . is not like the first time around. For one thing, it poses a new set of personal relationships to be established—with your ex-husband and in-laws, with your new husband's children and family, even, in many instances, with your own friends. Then, too, you ask yourself lots of questions that you somehow didn't ask the first time around. How do you tell your children you are going to get married? Can they participate in the ceremony? Can you wear white? A veil? Carry a traditional bridal bouquet? Do persons give you gifts at this time? For that matter, can you have a large, tradition-filled wedding and reception? In short, how much celebrating is within the boundaries of good taste?[8]

Her answer is that as much celebrating as the couple wants is acceptable. She points out that there are ways of remarrying that reflect tact and good taste. The essence of her advice is this: be yourself; do not try to hide the fact that it is a second marriage (and for this reason she discourages veils and white wedding gowns unless they have a touch of color added somewhere); and be sensitive to the feelings and needs of others.

The key elements that both of these books of etiquette seem to include are freedom and variety. One can feel free from the restraints one might have felt when parents were paying for the wedding; one is free to do what one wants to do and can afford to do in the wedding celebration. In the first marriage there were many traditions to which one conformed; in the new marriage the couple create their own traditions (not completely forgetting the old, of course).

The Minister's Contribution to the Remarriage Wedding

If the couple has faced their individual and paired readiness for marriage' and if they do not want an automatic wedding (a carbon copy of the first) and if they are ready to think about the meaning of a wedding and how to create a wedding that expresses their unique lifestyle, love, commitment, and relationship, then what a beautiful opportunity a minister has! The minister can help them prepare an unforgettable day that is the beginning of a maturing, growing relationship. What can the minister do? Several things.

The minister can take pains *not* to confer any "second class status" on remarriage weddings. If the minister chooses to enter into this event, she or he should do it enthusiastically. Too often the clergyperson seems to communicate the attitude "I guess this happens and you need clergy, but I don't need to be enthusiastic. We will do this ceremony quietly and quickly in this side room. Let's get it over with. Please, no happiness or celebration!" I propose that the minister take just the opposite stance. I propose that when discussing where the marriage is to take place, the minister tell the couple, "You may be married in the sanctuary, the chapel, the church parlor, your house, my house, someone else's house or some out-of-door setting that you cherish. *You* choose. From my perspective, you are welcome to any of them. If you want a reception at the church, the facilities and services of the church are available to you. You are welcome here. We want to support you in planning a lovely day, the prelude to an enduring relationship!"

I suggest that the minister back up such a statement by aiding the couple with whatever services they need in order to implement their decision, whether it is locating the musicians they want or using church objects such as candelabra, kneeling cushions, and so forth, to make the church a caring host to these persons entering remarriage.

The minister can be open to the new variety in weddings, particularly for remarriages. The clergyperson can help the couple find the resources to discover some of the possibilities and can help them direct their planning energies in appropriate directions.

I realize that I write as a clergy in the "free-church" tradition and as one who has especially claimed that heritage. Creating rituals that connect to ancient forms while expressing the newness of today is enriching beyond words, particularly when it occurs at the significant moments of one's life.

When a couple comes to me to be married, I often show them two books. One is a bound "little black book," the book of marriage ritual that I used at the beginning of my ministry. The other is the loose-leaf notebook that is my marriage manual today. I tell the couple that together we will create their wedding service.

I tell them that there are three essential elements in a wedding service: (1) it must include their vows to each other, which is the irreducible core; (2) it should be expressive of their unique life-style; (3) since it will be a service of worship, it should be reverent, respectful, filled with awe and wonder, invoking divine blessing.

I tell them that if planning a wedding overwhelms them, I will plan all of it from my conversation with them, all of it, that is, except for the vows, which I insist that they either select, edit, or write themselves.

I suggest that to prepare their vows each person separately think about and write down the answers to two questions: "What am I promising my partner when we marry?" and "What am I asking my partner when we marry?"

After they have answered these questions as completely as possible, then they each show their answers to the other and discuss them. If it is all right with the couple, there need not be unanimity as to what each is promising and asking.

As a next step, I suggest that the couple (individually or together) *either* write out these promises/expectations in the form of their covenant-vows and then look at a page of sample vows that I give them (some published and some created by other couples), *or* look first at the page of vows to see if any one of them comes close to what they want to say and then change or add to the wording to make it uniquely theirs.

While I use this process with persons entering first marriages as well as person entering second marriages, I am struck by a difference in the way couples approach this task. It seems to me that quite frequently the persons entering second marriages do this with more depth, perceptiveness, and enthusiasm. Recently, I was really impressed by the extremely careful, thoughtful statements of a promise/expectation that two persons, both entering a second marriage (with each other), brought to me. When I commented on how much thought and effort must have gone into this, the husband-to-be, a research scientist, told me that he had taken a day off just to think about his wedding vows and work on writing them. He gave this task that kind of priority.

Many remarrying persons are ready to move from the passive role of "being married" by the clergy to the active role of "marrying each other" with the clergy's counsel and support.

As I look at the statements the persons are developing in preparation for their wedding, I realize that a fresh counseling opportunity awaits me. For lack of a better term, I call it "convenantal counseling." I probe such questions as:

—Why did you put in that item? What did you choose to leave out? (Or I note items not mentioned, point them out, and ask the couple if they want these to be part of their covenant.)
—What promise will be the easiest to keep?

—What promise will be the most difficult to keep?

If the vows are too detailed, I discuss again with the couple the difference between contract and covenant. I leave the final decision to them as to what stays in and what comes out of the final statement of their vows.

I should be clear that the part I ask the couple to write is the stated wedding vow. The first part of the wedding vows, the betrothal vows, such as "Will you have this woman to be your wedded wife . . . ?" remains the responsibility of the minister. I never vary from asking people for a lifetime commitment in that vow. Though such a promise may prove difficult to keep, my understanding of my task as minister is that in all preparation, the wedding itself, and the support offered to the couple after the wedding, an enduring marriage bond is the goal.

The end results of this effort—the covenant-vows that the couple share at their wedding—then become the very heart of their wedding ceremony. I usually type them out clearly, double-spaced, on a page in that loose-leaf notebook, which I hold between the couple so that they can say their vows to each other. They do not need to repeat them after me and are freed from having to memorize the vows. There are exceptions, however. Some people are uneasy about reading aloud in front of others. Some second marriages take place between older people who have eye problems or wear bifocals. If they find reading difficult, I offer the vows phrase by phrase for them to repeat.

But to return to the subject of preparing the rest of the wedding service, I share with the couple an outline of the more frequently included elements in a wedding service.

    I. Processional
   II. Welcome, Bible readings, sermonette on marriage
 III. Parents' blessing
 IV. Vows
      A. Betrothal vows
      B. State vows
      C. Ring vows
  V. Prayer for the couple
 VI. Pronouncement
VII. Benediction
VIII. Recessional

I ask them to react to this outline and make any suggestions they desire. To this end, I lend them a copy of the book to which I referred earlier, *Write Your Own Wedding*, and depending on their religious heritage, perhaps a second resource, *Together for Life*, by Joseph M. Champlin.[9] (The latter book is a set of resources for the Catholic marriage rite.) And then we plan. In the parts of the service for which they do not have any suggestions, I attempt to prepare the service, guided by the sharing with one another that we have done in the counseling sessions.

Out of such planning, uniqueness in weddings does occur. One wedding took place early on a Sunday morning. A small group—only the couple's faith-support group and the bride's immediate family—gathered under a flowering apple tree in the yard of the bride's parents' home. After a simple, brief service, the group joined hands in a friend-ship circle around the couple and each person offered a sentence prayer on behalf of the couple. This circle of prayer was a custom from their faith-support group and took the place of the pastor's prayer for them. They then went inside to share a breakfast the bride's mother had prepared. Later, the whole group went to the church worship service together. During the service the couple announced their wedding and invited the entire congregation to share coffee and pastries after worship as a continued reception-celebration.

Another wedding took place in the sanctuary in a rather informal style. At one point in the service, three people came forward, one carrying a ceramic chalice, one carrying a loaf of bread, one carrying a jug of wine—all gifts made by the persons carrying them. These gifts were used for Communion. First the bride and groom and their extended families, including their children, came to receive Communion together, expressing the bonds of faith the couple felt as they merged their lives and invited their families to enter into this merger. Then the elements were offered to all present, served by the bride, groom, and pastor. Even for churches where Communion is not an essential part of every worship service, it may be an important part of some second marriage services. It is a symbol of forgiveness, of costly love, and of persons bound together in faith in the God who came in Christ. It is also a symbol of oneness emerging out of brokenness. The Lord's Supper may have powerful significance to the persons entering this marriage and to their guests.

Another wedding took place in the home of a friend of the groom. At one point in the wedding service, the couple welcomed the friends gathered there. Then those wedding guests had the opportunity to share their love, their hopes, and their prayers for the couple in a spirit of celebration and worship.

Still another couple chose a very private wedding service, with only the children of the groom and the bride's mother present. Then, a week later, they had a wedding celebration party at their church with special music, group singing, games, and "questions and answers" with the bride and groom.

In another example, there was a beautiful, late afternoon, formal, candlelight wedding. Practically everything seemed to resemble a first wedding, except that the bride appeared in a lovely flowered formal dress. In planning she explained, "My first wedding was when we were in military service in Europe. We had a civil ceremony and were whisked out of there so fast that we had to put our rings on each other on the sidewalk in front of the magistrate's office. It was not a dignified beginning to what I hoped would be an important relationship. This time I wanted my wedding to have beauty and dignity." And it did. The care given not only to the physical details but also to the wedding ceremony itself reflected the commitment and ideals of that bride and groom.

Each of these weddings was an appropriate expression of a particular bride and groom entering a new marriage. A couple's desire for variety can be guided so that the location, style, and size of wedding, the vows, and the ways in which reverence is expressed can be fitting expressions of those people entering the marriage relationship.

Another contribution of the minister can be to help the couple interpret the wedding to their children and other family members. The minister, when it is appropriate, can help the couple involve these persons in their wedding.

As the remarrying couple is probably well aware, they carry even more persons along with them into this marriage relationship than into the last one. Wise planning of a wedding, therefore, may include helping the children and other family members recognize the marriage and their place in it.

Let's talk about the children of the remarrying people. Ideally, a three-stage process would take place between a remarrying couple and their children: first, the couple would announce their wedding plans to their children; second, they would allow enough time between the announcement and the wedding for the children to absorb this news and ask questions about how the marriage will influence their lives (this time would enable the couple to overcome the children's resistance and gain their acceptance); third, in discussion with the children, the couple can plan ways for the children to be involved in the wedding. For example, depending on the children's ages, talents, and interests, children could be involved in the wedding as:

—flower girl, ring bearer;
—attendant to the bride or groom;
—usher;
—musician, instrumental or vocal;
—person who offers a reading at the wedding;
—person in charge of the guest book;
—one who makes the wedding cake, hosts the reception, or pins on the flowers.

Creative couples can discover ways to involve younger children as well. Perhaps the children can help make invitations or decorations, or perhaps the children can help plan the reception so that there are refreshments, people (including other children), and games and/or activities that they enjoy.

Or they could be involved in the vows. For example, some couples choose explicitly to mention each other's children by name during their wedding vows, along with their promise to care about those children and support the primary parent. There are doubtless other ways that children of bride or groom could be involved, but these are some suggestions.

There are also good reasons, however, why children often will not participate in such ways. If the children are minors and one's ex-spouse has custody, that ex-spouse may refuse to let the children attend the wedding. One remarried man told me that he wanted his children present at his wedding but his former wife refused. He said that he had been a "pleaser" all his life but that now he was in a circumstance in which he could not please his former wife, his children, the woman he wanted to marry, *and* himself. So he had to decide to proceed even though he missed his children's presence. His step of assertiveness did, in time, open the way for his children's acceptance of his new marriage.

Or the children themselves may have reasons why they do not want to participate. For one thing, a wedding is a visible sign that one's original parents are not going to get back together again! I know a junior-high-age girl who fainted while participating in her father's wedding. There was just too much evidence of her thwarted dreams and permanently changed future for her to absorb. Another child may feel that it is disloyal to the other parent to take part in one parent's wedding. Or the child may have enjoyed having the complete attention of the single parent and dread the intrusion of a stepparent.

For these reasons the children of the remarrying couple may be absent or very passive at the wedding. The pastor may need to help the couple deal with such attitudes as a foretaste of some of the issues they will face in marriage and as a test of their commitment to each other and their understanding of each other's life situations. The pastor may also have a ministering task with the children to help them accept the reality of what is happening in their lives and in the lives of their parents.

Couples need to be aware of two cautions about children's involvement in the wedding. One caution is that the adults should be very sensitive to the children's feelings, attitudes, and needs related to the coming wedding. A child should never feel forced to participate, and adults should be careful lest their own enthusiasm for the coming wedding make them unaware of the pressures that children may be feeling. The other caution is that children should not be allowed to dominate the wedding or to spoil it by keeping everyone in suspense about their participation. Even if children are invited to participate and agree to do so, there should be an alternate plan so that if they change their minds at the last minute, the wedding can go on with a minimum of trauma for both children and adults.

If it does not seem right to have children participate in the wedding, perhaps later there might be a "family-formation ceremony." This might be a more private and relaxed celebration in their own home, as the members of the new remarried family talk about their hopes and dreams together.

Yet another way to include children in the events surrounding the remarriage might be the planning of a "familymoon" (a honeymoon for the new family). This can include family-building activities and the creation of new family traditions.[10]

The question of people's involvement in the second wedding is broader than the question of the bride's and groom's children. The couple may also want to ask, "Who are the significant people in our lives—family members, friends, others who have influenced us—that we would like to be involved in our wedding in some way? How can we involve them?"

The minister can seek—even beyond the ways we have already mentioned—to let the wedding be an expression of "realized forgiveness," of "grace," and of the new beginnings that are possible in the Christian faith.

Perhaps explicit symbols of new beginnings will be included in the minister's message, the vows, and other places in the wedding. Some topics and symbols could include

—birth and re-birth of individuals and relationships;
—death and resurrection;
—butterflies, flowers, and rainbows;
—winter and spring;
—tears and laughter.

Perhaps the wedding will include such acted-out symbols of grace, forgiveness, and new beginnings as celebrating the Lord's Supper, lighting the unity candle, and stating and/or signing the marriage covenant. Perhaps through the previous counseling by the pastor and acceptance of the couple and their plans by the pastor, the forgiveness has become real, and so the wedding just *is*.

At any rate, perhaps remarrying people who come with their children, their families, and their histories are ready to make, as their own, the person-to-person promise that the widowed Ruth once made to her mother-in-law, Naomi:

> "Entreat me not to leave you or to return from following you; for where you go I will go, and where you lodge I will lodge; your people shall be my people, and your God my God; where you die I will die, and there I will be buried"(Ruth 1:16-17a).

Pastoral Care of the Remarried Couple After the Wedding

> This is what marriage means: helping one another to reach the full status of being persons, responsible and autonomous beings who do not run away from life.—Paul Tournier[1]

The church pastor, whose obedience to the Bible's one-flesh teaching about marriage means doing everything possible to help the remarriage succeed, has many opportunities to be of help after the wedding is over. Almost certainly the new couple will face many tasks and many issues in building their couple relationship and in establishing their reconstituted family. For the sake of discussion, we are going to separate the couple-building task from the family-building task, although, of course, both will need to go on simultaneously. The couple and the total family will intersect with and have an impact upon one another.

For now, we concentrate our attention on couple relationship. We will treat all other matters as though they are intrusions into the couple's life (and they may well be experienced as such by the couple at times). Then in the next chapter we will explore the family issues as legitimate concerns in their own right.

What Is the Couple's Task with Each Other in the First Few Years of Remarriage?

It appears to us that newly married persons must deal with at least four areas as they begin their remarried life together: (a) any residual grief and other unfinished business from their former relationships; (b) the usual tasks of newlyweds; (c) some increased tentativeness and lack of confidence about themselves as durable marriage mates, and about their relationship as a durable marriage union; and (d) complicating factors in the couple's environment.

Dealing with Residual Grief and Other Unfinished Business from the Former Relationship

We have spoken of the residue of grief in chapter 2. If that was not dealt with by each individual as completely as one might wish, it may surface as an extra item to deal with in the midst of other marriage tasks. Some tell us that though they thought they had left all that grief behind, it hits them again just before or just after beginning their second marriage. This grief may be unexpected, for they sense they should be feeling happy about the new life opening before them. Still, moving ahead and entering into a marriage relationship with another person is admission that the old relationship has really ended. The death or the divorce is real. Any subconscious fantasies that one day a reconciliation with the former spouse might take place need to be abandoned. And so grief may return to complicate the tasks of building a marriage partnership with a new person.

Dealing with the Usual Tasks of Newlyweds

The remarried couple has the usual tasks of newlyweds involved in building a life together. They need to work out together a number of tasks, including the following:

1. They need to discover what has changed as they move from a courtship relationship to a marriage relationship. There is a change of status to be sure. What else? For some the change feels like a change for the better; in marriage there may be commitment, intimacy, permanence, guilt-free sexual experience, companionship, partnership, support. For others, marriage may mean an overwhelming responsibility, something heavy added to what had been a light, playful relationship.

2. They need to discover what, if any, denial has been going on during the courtship. Laura Singer notes that premarriage behavior has much denial behavior.[2] This implies no intentional dishonesty on the part of either partner. But the effort to put one's best self forward tends to cause one to hide or deny certain dark parts of one's personality. Then, too, the changed circumstances may bring out other aspects of one's personality. Most married persons, including remarried persons, admit to some surprises about the person they married. "I never saw his rage. . . . I never saw her difficulty with alcohol. . . . I never saw

his tenseness around children. . . . I never saw his or her spendthrift side. . . . I never saw his or her stingy side. . . .'' Recognizing and accepting these unknown aspects of a new spouse and learning how to come to terms with them are big, important tasks for the newlywed. It is also important for them to know that such surprises are widespread, and so they need not feel stupid or guilty that they didn't "really know" their partner before marriage.

3. The newlywed couple need to learn to deal with the differences between two people, their different needs, their different wants. What do they want of each other in regard to sharing of necessary household work? What do they want of each other in regard to money? What would they like their partner to do for them? (Some men like their wives to pick out their clothes and some women enjoy similar help; others consider this meddling.) We'll speak of some of the major issues for remarried couples shortly.

4. The newlywed couple may need to learn to deal with dissimilar needs for intimacy and closeness. Many marital conflicts, especially early ones, are about "optimal distance," whether the members of the couple know it or not. How much feeling of closeness can each stand? How much time does each want to spend with the other? How much privacy and alone time does each need? Can these needs be stated, recognized, accepted? Some couples report arguments that bewilder them, arguments that break out after their most intimate times—for example, right after a delightful sexual experience. It may be that this is the expression of either or both needing to establish their distance again.

5. In a similar vein, the newlywed couple need to learn to distinguish between togetherness and closeness. Some couples believe that a sign of closeness (deep rapport and caring about each other) is constant togetherness. Therefore, they believe that they should attempt to do everything together, or as much as they possibly can. Dr. Singer suggests,

> . . . yearning for sameness is really a distorted concept of marriage and the meaning of married love. . . . [It is] unrealistic and inappropriate to the marriage. The striving for oneness between husband and wife stifles individuality and creates a sense of being choked, trapped and overwhelmed by too much closeness and togetherness.[3]

She points out that togetherness is a physical fact, while closeness is an emotional perception. Separate activities—particularly if one partner loves the activity and the other doesn't but is quite happy to grant the partner the freedom to pursue it—can contribute to closeness in a marriage. Of course, the constant search in marriage is for a balance between separate activities and together activities, so that both personal interests and the life of the couple are nurtured. Some togetherness and much closeness is the goal.

6. Yet another task of the newlywed couple is to discover what love will and will not do. One of the basic problems of marriage in our society is that our society bases the marriage relationship almost completely on love and then imposes demands on this love that it can never fulfill, such as these:

"If you love me, you won't do anything without me."
"If you love me, you'll do what I say."
"If you love me, you'll give me what I want."
"If you love me, you'll know what I want before I ask."[4]

Expectations like these become a sort of emotional blackmail that people sometimes unknowingly use on their spouses. A basic task early in the marriage is for the partners to move from unrealistic love to realistic love instead of to cynicism or a sense of betrayal.

7. Another task of the newlywed couple is to work out the dynamics of power in their relationship. Who has what power? How do partners influence each other? How is power balanced? Many marriage theorists feel that unless the power issue is faced and worked through, intimacy can be only superficial.[5]

There are probably more tasks for those beginning a remarriage, but this list has described some of them.

Dealing with Self as a Durable Marriage Mate and the Relationship as a Durable Marriage Union

Building a good marriage is a delicate task, and it is all the more delicate for remarried people because they may come to the task with some increased tentativeness about themselves as durable mates and the marriage relationship as a lasting union. As a pastor I have seen a number of people seek remarriage with a romantic "love conquers all" attitude. There are the persons who might say, "My former spouse was apathetic to me, but this one is attentive. I couldn't talk with my former spouse, but with this person I can talk out anything that I want to. My former spouse was indifferent to our children, but this one has already become more of a father/mother than my former spouse ever was," and so forth. Such a person will probably have a shock sometime in the future when he or she discovers that his or her new spouse is fairly human and that he or she was in love with an illusion of the person, not with the real person.

As much as a person enjoys the new marriage partner, there are still some lurking fears. Mel Krantzler speaks of "remarriage shock."[6] Mel experienced such shock. He and the woman he married, Pat, had been living together and thought that they felt ready for the commitment of marriage. To their amazement, on their wedding day they felt, not exhilarated, but nauseated, dizzy, and fatigued. For days after their wedding ceremony they sensed they were suddenly strangers with each other. They felt tense, awkward, clumsy around each other. It took a number of days before they started to be to each other what they had been before that wedding ceremony.[7] The fear of commitment, the awareness of how much it would hurt if this relationship failed, the loss/change of personal roles—all these factors and more entered into Mel and Pat's severe case of remarriage shock.

Not all couples will react as strongly as Mel and Pat did to their remarriage, but many will understand some of the fears that brought on that reaction. One remarried woman told us, "Whenever my husband and I have problems, I find myself panicking. He doesn't threaten or anything, but I find myself imagining him leaving. I try to think how I could make it without him. Our relationship is polluted by my fear of abandonment."

Many things can contribute to a couple's growing confidence and trust that their relationship is rich and strong and will endure: the passage of time, the reassurance and support of pastor and friends, the couple's letting each other know how much they treasure the relationship, rich experiences as a couple and as a family, surviving a time of tension or conflict, surviving a crisis together.

Dealing with Complicating Factors in the Couple's Environment

There is still one other matter that complicates the remarried couple's building their new marriage bond: factors in their societal environment. The fact of remarriage may create some pressures on the couple. Some of the elements in their lives that would normally provide a supportive and an encouraging environment may be resistant to a second marriage. Some of these pressures are external, such as these.

—The neighborhood or community in which the couple lives is

nonaccepting. If one partner moves into the house of a new spouse, neighbors may have a hard time accepting the newcomer.

—Parents, in-laws, and former in-laws express resistance.

—Some institutions (schools, churches, hospitals) show a great deal of insensitivity. For example, there may be carelessness about names, lack of recognition of the fact that family members may have different last names, or lack of recognition of stepparents as concerned adults able to make decisions for their stepchildren.

—Folklore and mass media, the powerful image makers among the institutions of society, have not provided a very supportive or helpful view of remarried families.

—The law also creates some difficulties, including the lack of legal rights of the stepparent.

There are also internal pressures that complicate the new couple's task, such as these.

—Differences in faith, values, and life-style affect both the couple and the children of both persons.

—Previous bonds that existed before the couple's relationship include one's own children, one's former in-laws, and friends from the former marriage(s).

—Relationships with ex-spouses may continue to interfere.

—Discipline problems, resistance, and divisiveness of children and stepchildren emerge.[8]

The most constant and most important factor in the new couple's environment is the presence of children of one or both spouses who need attention for themselves and need to be helped to adjust to their parents' new relationship. We will speak of this in more detail in the next chapter.

All of these adjustment tasks are part of the couple's early years together. And there is more to come! Starting with the first months of marriage and proceeding through their years together, the remarried couple has several important tasks.

They must create a family, which will not be the old family it used to be, but a new family. They will need to pick and choose from the previous family methods, styles, heritages, and traditions. They will become a new family with its own rituals, celebrations, traditions, and memories.

The couple will need to deal with a myriad of questions and issues involving the children. What do children and stepparents call each other? How does a parent draw another adult into the parenting task? How, who, what, when should they discipline? How does each adult deal with the rivalries and the resistances that the children may well carry on for years?

The partners will need to develop their own style in money management. They may well both bring financial assets and liabilities from their previous lives to this marriage. Either or both partners may have financial obligations that they need to pay (for example, child support), and they may receive child-support money or income from other persons. There may be lots of battles and tension here. Child-support money sent from outside dilutes a stepparent's authority. Child-support money sent elsewhere diminishes a stepparent's resources for the new family. But both may be realities that the partners need to face and live with. A man may feel the conflict acutely when his former wife and biological children compete with his present wife and stepchildren for what income he has. As a result, either or both partners within a remarriage may feel so burned by financial settlements from their previous marriages that they choose to be secretive about their finances. Openness and honesty about finances may need to be developed. If both have income, they need to work out how they will operate with two incomes and who pays for what. The money issues in remarriage are particularly complicated, and there are many aspects of the subject with which to deal. Consistently, when remarried persons list their most important problems, children and money finish first and second.

Since each partner has his or her own distinct history and, thus, his or her own distinct needs, each needs to be good at negotiating differences. A couple need to know how to manage their conflicts. It is quite probable that they will need to "unlearn" some habits and learn some new methods for dealing with conflict. Many remarried people are extremely uneasy with arguing and conflict, for it reminds them of the painful, unsuccessful arguments that were part of the terminating of their previous marriage. The trust and courage to admit anger, the ability to confront a valued marriage partner with something troubling both of them, skill in talking things out until they have identified the issue and looked for possible solutions, and the persistence to keep working until a tentative solution is reached and tried—such are the cement that can hold a marriage together and make a good marriage great. But such skills are the ones that many remarried people feel they don't possess and are thus skills that they may be hesitant and fearful of trying. And so the remarried couple has the twin dilemma of needing great negotiating skills because they face many issues early in their marriage and, at the same time, feeling very uneasy about their conflict-management and negotiating skills. This may be an area in which the newly remarried couple needs much aid and assistance.

The Marriage Contract

Clifford Sager and associates have developed the method of analyzing a couple's life together in terms of what they call "the marriage contract." This does not refer to formal written documents or agreements, but rather to the conscious and unconscious expectations that each partner has of the relationship. This contract exists on three levels of awareness: (1) verbalized—those aspects that have been talked out (although they may not have been heard, understood, or accepted by the receiver); (2) conscious but not verbalized—those expectations of which one partner is aware but which have not been expressed or discussed with his or her spouse; (3) beyond awareness or unconscious—those that are very much a part of a person but of which he or she may not even be aware. This third level usually becomes an awareness when one experiences a thought, feeling, or uneasiness that something is not right.

Sager notes that there are three areas on which such a marriage contract operates:

A. Expectations of the Marriage
1. A mate committed to a lifelong, romantic, intimate, loyal, devoted, and exclusive relationship
2. Help with care and discipline of children
3. Companionship and escape from loneliness and the singles' scene
4. Escape from burdens, strife, and chaos in one's life
5. Sanctioned, guilt-free, available sex
6. Bearing a child with the new marital partner
7. A relationship that includes family life and parenting as well as the marital pairing
8. The hope that the spouse will include children, former friends, ex-in-laws in the allowed list of continuing contacts
9. A financial plan that either merges everything or keeps financial resources separate
10. Membership in a social unit that contributes to one's sense of purpose in life

11. A ready-made family

12. The chance to be taken care of by a strong mother/father figure

13. The opportunity to prove that one is desirable to one's former spouse

14. The opportunity to rescue a struggling individual and possibly that person's children

B. Psychological and Biological Needs

1. One's relationships with one's children. Are parents and children inappropriately close? Is there a place for a new spouse?

2. Ties to one's ex-spouse. Has "emotional divorce" taken place? Are there residual feelings of either hostility/revenge or affection?

3. Independence/dependence. What style has one evolved as a single person? How will this be continued/adapted in the new relationship?

4. Activity/passivity, closeness/distance, use/abuse of power, dominance/submission. What style has one evolved in these areas during single life? How will this be continued/adapted in the new relationship?

5. Guilt. Does either partner live with such a load of guilt that it influences behavior toward children, parents, ex-in-laws, or former spouse?

6. Roles in parenting. What role does each expect of self and partner in regard to parenting and stepparenting?

7. Fear of abandonment or loneliness. Has fear of being abandoned or lonely entered into mate choice, interactions, or lack of interactions in this couple?

8. Control. Does either feel the need to control and possess one's spouse? Is this a repetition of a former relationship?

9. Anxiety. How relaxed or how anxious is each partner about this relationship? How is the anxiety expressed?

10. Defensiveness. How does each partner express defensiveness to the other?

11. Gender identity. How does each partner feel about his or her gender identity?

12. Sex. What characteristics does each partner desire in his or her sex partner? What satisfactions or what discomforts are experienced here?

13. Acceptance. Do both express acceptance of self and of the other?

14. Cognitive style. How similar/dissimilar are the couple in cognitive style, in the way each takes in information, processes it, decides about it, and communicates conclusions? Are the partners complementary in this regard?

C. External Foci of Marital Problems

1. Communication. Are the two open with each other? Can they talk and negotiate differences?

2. Life-style. What life-style and cultural similarities or differences are experienced?

3. Families. How does each feel about the partner's style of relating to his or her family of origin? Likewise, how does each feel about the partner's way of relating to ex-spouse and ex-in-laws?

4. Children. What are their agreements and their conflicts around child rearing, discipline, and relationships with both one's biological children and one's stepchildren?

5. "Family myths." Does this couple maintain "family myths," unrealistic evaluations by family participants of the quality of their life together (myths may describe former marriages or this one).

6. Finances. Are money matters worked out satisfactorily?

7. Celebrations and holidays. Has the couple worked out family milestones and holidays? Who will attend children's celebrations? Where will children spend holidays, etc.? Are plans acceptable to all?

8. Sexuality. Is the couple comfortable with their own sexual relationship and with what they communicate to their children about sexuality? Do they understand the concept of the weakened incest taboo? (See p. 99 for a further discussion of this.)

9. Value questions. Is there general agreement about values involving money, culture, ethics, relationships, religious beliefs, religious practices, use of time? What needs to be discussed and negotiated?

10. Friends. What is each partner's attitude toward and treatment of the other's friends? Are friends from each partner's past allowed?

11. Roles. What roles seem fitting—gender-based roles or flexible roles?

12. Interests. Are interests shared or not? Are differences in interest respected or resented?

13. Socioeconomic class. How similar/dissimilar are the socio-economic classes from which each marriage partner comes? Will this create problems for children who may need to move from one class to another when visiting the other parent?[9]

Consciously and unconsciously, a couple is developing and evolving a marriage contract as they build their life together.

Behavior Profile

Sager notes that during the process of evolving their marriage contract, a couple is also developing what he calls their "behavior profile"—that is, their style of relating, behaving, and adapting to each other. He notes that there are seven behavior profiles that may emerge.

1. *Equal partners* relate in a cooperative, independent manner and basically seek equality for oneself and for the partner. They do not cling or lean but are capable of sustained intimacy. Each can assume decision making and give the partner the freedom to do the same.

2. *The romantic partner* is quite dependent on one's mate and feels incomplete without him or her. Anniversaries and sentiment are very important to the romantic partner. Though romantic partners may have a satisfying marriage, Sager offers the caution that such partners may tend to ignore children and other responsibilities because they are completely wrapped up in themselves.

3. *The parental partner* treats one's mate like a child and is perhaps mildly patronizing, controlling, or authoritative.

4. *The childlike partner*, on the other hand, wants to be guided, disciplined, and taken care of.

5. *The rational partner* aspires to a well-ordered, reasonable, logical relationship with his or her spouse. Responsibilities need to be nego-tiated and clearly defined. There may well be a close, emotionally meaningful relationship, but the rational partner finds it difficult to acknowledge the importance of emotions or express them.

6. *The companionate partner,* as the name implies, seeks a com-panion. Romantic love may not be a part of this person's expectation. Passion may not be important, but the person would like not to be lonely and is willing to offer thoughtfulness, loyalty, and kindness and hopes to receive such considerations in return. This person may want the companionship of married life but be afraid to love again.

7. *The parallel partner* attempts to have his or her life run parallel rather than intertwine with that of a marital partner. This person avoids

intimate relationships. All the forms of an intimate home may be maintained, but real intimacy is avoided. Distance and emotional space are needs that the parallel partner experiences.[10]

It is helpful for a couple to examine each partner's behavior profile to discover if this is the way one wants to relate and if this is the type of relationship for which the partner hopes. If not, the couple need to explore how the relationship can be reordered. Can the couple achieve this reordering or do they need assistance?

Stages of Development

Of course, none of what we have described remains static. A couple's relationship evolves through time. So we go on to look at the couple's life from yet another perspective, the stages of their development.

As the remarried couple deals with the issues we have mentioned, they will proceed through certain stages in their couple development. Susan Campbell has described the couple's journey quite reliably (though she readily admits that it is an inaccurate roadmap because it fits no one couple perfectly) when she speaks of five stages through which a couple may pass. She suggests that the first stage is "Romance," when the partners are inspired by visions, illusions, fantasies, sheer enjoyment, and delight in each other's presence. The couple's task at this point is to discover their shared possibilities and visions. They need to avoid the pitfall of falling into the illusion that wishing makes it so. This stage ends when the couple sense that it is not going to be as easy as they had imagined, and they move on to the second stage, the "Power Struggle." Each partner discovers that the other is not exactly what he or she had imagined, nor is their life as a couple what he or she had dreamed. In this stage a couple experience differences, difficulties, disillusionment, disappointment, anger. They discover that there are many conflicts of needs and interests that will need to be faced and managed.

The third stage is called "Stability" and begins with forgiveness and with the ability to let up on the power struggle as each begins to accept the other person as he or she is. Partners come to accept the other as an individual person, with his or her own dreams, strengths, foibles, weaknesses, and failures. They discover that they can learn and progress from their conflicts.

The fourth stage, "Commitment," occurs when the couple accept and surrender to what is. They give up trying to reform each other and no longer feel the need to be agreeable at all costs. They discover that they can challenge each other and conflict with each other without being locked into the power struggle. They can build an enriching life together. The pitfall is that the couple may concentrate on their inner harmony so exclusively that they do not sense the need to concern themselves also with the world beyond.

The fifth stage ''Co-Creation'' is when a couple take all that they have learned in building their own relationship and attempt to apply it to the world in some way, for they sense that the richness is to be shared, that they are intermingled with the world as co-creators of the world yet to be. And so they discover how to nurture their own relationship and how to give of themselves out of the overflow.[11]

The remarried couple may proceed through Campbell's stages of a couple's journey, but with complications. For one thing, either or both may bring families with them. The remarried couple starts earlier than their families in building their relationship, and they do so with more choice, intention, and enthusiasm. Thus, the new family members coming together may go through the stages much more slowly and be more resistant to change than the couple would have hoped. Further, the day-to-day decisions that we have discussed about finances, children's discipline and needs, and so forth, bring an early note of realism to the remarried couple's relationship. These decisions, combined with a couple's probable unease in handling conflict, may cause a remarried couple to come to Campbell's second stage, ''Power Struggle,'' sooner and stay in it longer than couples who come to their relationship with less responsibilities beyond themselves.

The remarried couple seeking to build their life together may find many barriers on the fourth and fifth stages ''Commitment'' and ''Co-Creation.''

What Can the Support Clergy and Other Church Leaders Offer a Remarried Couple?

The first gift the minister and other church leaders can offer to the couple is awareness. The issues and processes described so far in this chapter do not exaggerate what many remarried couples face in the early years of their marriage. It is a known fact that 40 percent of all remarriages terminate in the first four years. Such a statistic is, at the very least, an indication of the huge tasks and tremendous stresses that newly remarried couples may encounter.

This awareness of and sensitivity to the difficulty of early remarriage might take many forms:

—The minister or church leaders could simply observe the couple for signs of happiness, joy, strain, or trouble.

—A couple who has been successfully remarried for a period of time could have the remarried couple over for dinner or take them out to dinner. Sometime during the evening they might say something like, "Things are much better now, but we really had a struggle in the early years of our remarriage. Some of the things that really gave us problems were. . . . We're hoping for the best with you. How's it going?"

—The minister or church leaders could involve the couple and children/stepchildren in couple, family, and children's activities of the church. This would give the church leaders a chance to be sensitive to what this new family is experiencing.

Second, the clergy can offer the newly remarried couple at least two specific, intentional contacts. We suggest that these be spoken of in the premarriage counseling sessions, if the clergy is so fortunate as to be able to work with the couple before the wedding. (If not, the same sort of sensitivities and intentional support of remarried couples should still prevail.) In premarriage counseling, the clergy can suggest the importance of the first year and ask if he or she can have a session with the couple after three months, after six months, and again shortly after their first anniversary. Then the clergy should take the initiative to call the couple and set a date for a time when they can talk, perhaps in their home or in his or her office.

The clergy will want to have some very specific objectives for these two (or more) sessions. The first might be to establish or reestablish rapport, caring, and support for the couple and their life together. It is good for them to know that, with all the issues and tension in their lives, there is someone who is really pulling for them. If this is a couple at whose wedding the clergy officiated, the couple and clergy may want to share memories, not only of the wedding but also of the preparation. Quite probably in those premarriage sessions, the minister raised a number of issues that the couple thought would be no problem. An amazing amount of optimism and denial goes on in premarriage counseling sessions. The minister might recall the issues they discussed and ask the couple's perspective on them from the other side of the wedding. In this meeting the pastor might want to diagnose and help the couple diagnose how they are doing at this stage of their marriage. Couples may be well aware of some issues but think that they are alone. They may find it reassuring that many other couples face the same issues. The couple may be helped to recognize and claim what they value.

Perhaps the conversation will flow easily and come rather quickly to issues that trouble the couple, but the clergy might have a list of problem areas to suggest to the couple to see if they feel the need to talk about them. From our discussion in the preceding pages, that list might include these questions:

1. Has each partner recovered from previous love relationships and/ or marriages? Is there appropriate emotional distance from the persons involved in these relationships? Does the spouse accept the fact of the previous marriage and any continuing ties or responsibilities?

2. How are the partners doing on the early tasks of their marriage?

3. How are they doing in dealing with their tentativeness, their anxieties about making this marriage work? When does the relationship feel strongest? When does it feel weakest?

4. What outside supporting factors are contributing to their successful marriage? What outside factors are inhibiting it?

5. What issues of children, discipline, and family organization remain to be successfully dealt with? (More on this in the next chapter.)

6. Have the couple achieved a mutually satisfying agreement in regard to money and resource management? What is it? How was it achieved? If not, what steps can be taken to achieve greater harmony in money matters?

7. Do they have matters about which they are now in conflict? Would they like to work at solving some of those conflicts? Would they like to work at a process for conflict management as well?

8. What is their "marriage contract?" (Sager and associates place in counselees' hands a copy of the issues in a marriage contract and invite them either to discuss or to write out what they feel their contract is and bring their conclusions in to discuss with a counselor. This might be a method that clergy would find useful. Sager's suggested contract is more extensive and has more instructions than the brief summary we have included in this chapter.

a. Does either partner have contradictory wishes within the contract? (Probably no one is completely consistent.)

b. Does either feel that the partner is not fulfilling part of the contract? If so, what part? Can it be discussed and negotiated?

c. Has either partner changed the contract without telling the other? (Sometimes people make unrealistic promises before marriage, such as "Since I love you, I'll love your kids and they'll love me" or "We're going to become one big happy family; things will get back the way they used to be and ought to be." When the realities of married living bear down, these promises cannot be kept and resentment may set in.)

d. Has the contract changed with the couple's knowledge but with at least one person's resistance? (Some couples marry with the agreement that they will not have any children of this union. Sometimes at the urging of one partner, this agreement changes, causing problems for the other. This is but one example of a changed marriage contract.)

e. Can the couple work together toward the goal of having one conscious, articulated contract to which they both assent?

9. What "behavior profile" has each partner selected? Does it feel right to oneself? to one's partner? Does this need to be re-examined and/or renegotiated?

10. What stage has the couple reached in its journey as a married couple? Are they comfortable at that stage, or are they struggling to move on, to progress? What barriers are standing in their way? How can they get around these barriers?

11. It is our hunch that this question needs to be explored, whatever the clergy does with the other ten. How important is this couple relationship to each partner? How are the partners dealing with the competition for each other's love/loyalty, the competition from children, family, and others? Do they have an appropriate first commitment to each other? One of the convictions to which we authors return again and again is that the couple commitment needs to be basic. Without the commitment to keep together in spite of some difficulties, the remarried family can become two injured single-parent families rather quickly. Of course, there is the alternate danger that the couple get so wrapped up with each other that they ignore the needs of children and family. Sensitizing couples to make their couple commitment their first commitment and helping couples to recognize and deal with the competitions for that commitment can be a most valuable service indeed.

Because of the clergy's awareness of these issues, the initial contacts may grow into a longer-term counseling relationship. Length, terms, and goals may need to be discussed and worked out.

What we are suggesting here is early intervention. Thus, educative and preventative counseling can take place. It is probable that many remarrying couples will welcome such a pastoral offering during the early years of their marriage. If they do not feel the need, the door open to them in case of future need will in all probability be welcome also.

Should the clergy see the couple together or separately? Methods will differ. Probably most clergy will see the couple together a large part of the time. If the pastoral counselor senses one partner holding back, unable to articulate thoughts and feelings to the other partner, separate sessions may be indicated for at least one time.

In addition to awareness and personal contact, the clergy can offer to the couple the resources of the community. It is good to be informed about what educational groups, support groups, and counseling services are available for remarried persons in one's area so that appropriate referrals can be made.

Even more explicitly than has already been suggested, the clergy can involve the couple in their own diagnosis and treatment. The couple can participate in many ways:

—reading good material about remarriage, stepfamilies or particular issues (a bibliography is suggested in chapter 7);
—keeping a journal on their evolving life together;
—discussing and preparing an explicit marriage contract from the possibilities mentioned above;
—scheduling explicit couple times and family times and maintaining an awareness of their time needs.

The clergy's focus should be on encouraging the couple to work consciously at developing their own strength.

A difficult question for clergy is when to refer a couple or individual to another counselor. One guiding question might be this: Realizing that most couples experience stress and turmoil early in their remarriage, do I think that this current stress is *developmental* (having to do with working out problems in a rather complex setting) or is it *pathological* (having to do with some deep disturbance either in one partner or in their relationship)? It is our contention that a clergyperson can become well enough informed about remarriage to help persons through their developmental turmoil. However, unless one has had training beyond that of most of us (we are general practitioners in the field of counseling, with special offerings in religious insight), the pathological individuals and relationships should be referred to someone with in-depth professional training in the field of counseling. Mentally-ill persons, abusive persons, persons with character disorders, sexual deviates, chronic alcoholics, or persons who abuse other substances should, in all likelihood, be referred to specialists while the clergy maintains pastoral, caring relationships with those persons.

Beyond that, it is much more difficult to decide. If there are highly skilled counselors in your community who are willing to consult and advise you on how to treat this couple and how to recognize the matters that you cannot help, they would provide a valuable resource in such decision making.

There is a wide variety of help available for remarried persons. Some communities have rich counseling resources. In other communities, only clergy and family physicians are available. Whatever the community's circumstances, the clergy should know what resources are available and use them to contribute to the health and meaningfulness of marriages.

Before referring remarried couples and their families to a counselor or agency, the clergy should know that individual's or that agency's attitude toward stepfamilies. One of our consultants points out that many agencies still view the stepfamily as pathological. She was part of a social-work research group in a large western city. The group discovered that many agencies in that city do not recognize or understand stepfamilies. Ill-informed counselors are apt to treat developmental issues in stepfamilies as though they are pathological issues. Therefore, she counsels, check out the agency or therapist before referring.[12]

Later in the book we will discuss how the clergy can mobilize the resources of the church and offer these resources to the couple. In this chapter we have described how the clergy has the opportunity to make a limited but valuable contribution to the life of the remarried couple. R. Lofton Hudson puts it well:

> Just as the minister takes responsibility not for saving people but only of giving witness to the saving grace of God, so in counseling he takes responsibility not for saving a marriage but only for providing a relationship where two people can understand themselves better and learn better ways of relating to each other.[13]

Pastoral Care of the Remarried Family After the Wedding

> Unlike the young, who come to each other relatively empty-handed, the divorced [or widowed] man and divorced [or widowed] woman come with all the acquisitions of the years—their individual histories, habits, and tastes, their children, friends, and chattels. Love can be a rickety vehicle, loaded with so much of life's baggage.—Morton Hunt[1]

A couple entering remarriage has a more difficult time adjusting because often either or both bring children with them. The families of the remarrying persons find their lives complicated by the decision of these two people to marry. The clergyperson who wants to aid in strengthening remarried families must not only pay attention to the remarrying couple but also be sensitive to what is happening to the members of the remarrying families.

We shall begin with a brief overview of the issues dealing with family structure and children in the first years after marriage. We shall go on to mention some of the long-term issues that remarried families may face. And then we shall explore what the clergyperson can do to offer pastoral care to families with these experiences.

The Structure of the Remarried Family

The remarried family is a system with subsystems and a suprasystem! Contemporary family therapists speak of the family as a system; that is, it is a network of personal interactions, transactions, roles, rules, rituals, and mutual influences that all contribute to a family's being more than the sum of its parts.[2]

Family therapists approach a family that has an individual member with a problem by seeing the whole family as the patient, by identifying their counterproductive methods of dealing with each other, and by aiding the family to heal itself by discovering, experimenting with, and finding new ways to deal with one another.

The troubled remarried family is difficult to describe, diagnose, and treat, for in a remarried family two former family systems (now sub-systems) have come together. And yet, particularly in the early months of a remarried family, each previous family remains very much a system in itself, interacting with one another and trying to come to grips with this other system that is constantly present.

As if this were not complex enough, through the children of either spouse, this new remarried-family system is related to a much larger and more complex suprasystem, which includes former spouses, former spouses' spouses and children, former in-laws, aunts, uncles, grand-parents, and so on.

But let's go on and look at this from other perspectives.

The remarried family (often called ''stepfamily'') is an ''unfinished institution.'' We are using the term ''institution'' here in the sociological sense, referring to those enduring, predictable behaviors that society prescribes within any relationship. Marriage and the original family are ''finished insititutions.'' There is quite a clear understanding of what ''husband,'' ''wife,'' ''father,'' and ''mother'' are and how they are to behave. Although a good bit of variety is permitted, the parameters are relatively distinct. In contrast, the roles of the remarried-family members are not nearly so clear. This can be seen in the issue of names. What do persons in a remarried family call each other? How do they introduce each other? What is their new family unit called? Some terms are ''stepfamily'' (the prefix ''step'' has connotations of grief), ''re-constituted family,'' ''blended family,'' ''reconstructed family.'' Many remarried families don't feel comfortable with any of these terms but don't know a more fitting term.

What are the roles within the remarried family? We know what a ''mother'' is, but what is a ''stepmother''? Is she a wicked, cruel, power-grabbing person as portrayed in many fairy tales? Or is she a caring person who is due respect and caring, perhaps even love? What is a stepfather? Is he the inept, powerless, withdrawn, absent person portrayed sometimes in contemporary literature? Or is he a person with human strengths and weaknesses but with special gifts to bring to the new family and the persons within? And how does the family operate?

Who makes rules? Who enforces them? Who has that right?

And what about the roles of children in stepfamilies? How is a child supposed to relate to as many as four parental adults? What does one do with stepbrothers or stepsisters? A child may discover that his or her place among the children of the family changes. An only child may suddenly be one of several children. A youngest child may become a middle child. The children may have real role issues also.

Persons in the remarried family may find themselves struggling with issues which they thought they had resolved. The problem is that the answers to certain questions in one setting are not necessarily the right answers to the same questions in a different setting. New families will have to work out these issues for themselves because first marriages and intact families are finished institutions and remarriages and step-families are unfinished institutions. If a stepfamily ever becomes a finished institution, it will be because of that family's intentional efforts to make roles and expectations very clear.

Varying family heritages compete in the establishment of this new family life-style. It is not enough that the new family has to develop a life-style with little cultural guidance but various members of the family have competing memories as to what that life-style should be.

It has long been noted that even in first marriages both husband and wife bring family "legacies" with them. They have a set of memories, learned behavior, things they need, and things they treasure from their families of origin. But when two previously married persons and their children come together, there are six heritages that come together:

—each partner's family of origin;
—each partner's first-marriage family;
—each partner's single-parent household, which existed after death/divorce dissolved the first marriage and until this one was contracted.

And so there may be at least six opinions on "when to go to bed, where to put the television, how to light a fire, bake cookies, make pancakes, drive a car, and celebrate holidays."[3]

Such issues will come up almost hourly when two families begin their merging process. What about food, pets, work assignments, TV, radio and record players, church participation, religious observances in the home, temperature of the house, energy usage, etc., etc., etc.? Decisions by persons representing six previous family heritages will have to be made.

Remarried families will need to deal with the issue of space and territoriality. Will one individual and possibly that person's family move into the other's house? If so, will one family feel like guests (wanted or unwanted) and the other family feel "invaded or imposed upon"? How can such feelings be avoided? Since both marrying persons may have a fully furnished dwelling, whose furnishings will be used? In what combination? If there are residential children from both parents, does some sort of room-sharing agreement need to be worked out? Who decides what the arrangement will be?

Many persons feel that although it is not always feasible, there is wisdom in both families moving into a new home together. The new family can make choices about what dwelling it will be, what the function of rooms will be, who will share which room, what furnishings they will bring from both of their old homes, and what new furnishings they will add. While working out these decisions, wise partners know that each family member is asking the question "Where is my space?" in more than the typical housing sense, and so the couple will attempt to be sensitive in helping each person find his or her space.

The couple will want to assure their "space" as well. Some couples reserve for themselves the most private bedroom. They equip it with a sitting area and a lock on the door. Further, they communicate to children that there are times when they need to be alone in their room and not disturbed except for emergencies.

To put a previously discussed matter in a slightly different framework: in stepfamilies there is a wider involvement with more people. Less control and more interrelatedness, less power and more negotiating, less independence and more interdependence exist in stepfamilies than in intact families. Coauthor Carole recently told a bank official, "I'm Carole Della Pia-Terry, and I'd like to open a new account here." The bank official responded to her name by saying, "That sounds more like a corporation than a person!" Carole recalls, "He spoke more accurately than he knew. There are thirty-one people who own a piece of me. And those are just the main ones. There are many more minor characters in this family structure." One remarried husband put it this way, "I realized my wife came as a package, but I didn't realize the size of the package." And another said, "I didn't marry my wife, I married a crowd."

As some observers put it, while the boundaries of an intact family are quite clear, this is not so with a remarried family. The adults may feel that only they and their children are part of the family. But the children may have different definitions of family, which include all the caring adults and their children. The boundaries are not clear. Quite likely the children will from time to time move from one family unit to another, from one part of their family to the other part. Thus, both households will have to deal with each other on a variety of matters— schedules, holidays, finances, and decisions concerning the child's welfare (medical care, education, camping, music lessons/instruments, to name a few).

But the interaction of adults (at least two of whom were formerly married to each other) will be more complicated than that. Two sets of parents may have quite different standards, values, and styles in dealing with the child, and the child will have to move from one to the other. Parental adults need at least to understand the differences. Sadly, sometimes these former spouses still see each other as enemies and (perhaps without knowing it) cast their children in the role of spies. Adults may not be aware that they are doing it, but they may put on the children who move back and forth between families the burden for the jealousies, rivalries, and resentments that they still harbor toward one another. When parents cast their children as spies, they give the children tremendous power to play one parent against the other and also place much pressure on the children.

The complicated network created by the unresolved feelings that come from severed relationships may contribute to some particularly thorny problems with which remarried families must deal.

To be a bit more specific about one aspect of all this, we observe that members of a remarried family who are present in the household do not stay constant. They come and go. One husband in a remarried family suggested that if he were to symbolize their family life, he would put a revolving door in their house! Children for whom a couple has custody may spend regular weekends or vacations with the other parent. Children for whom the other parent has prime responsibility may arrive for short visits or extended vacation periods.

An increasing pattern is joint custody, with each biological parent having the children for equal amounts of time in a regularly alternating period. For some remarried families these alternating living arrangements are fairly predictable and stable. In others they are far from settled and stable. Children may play one parent against another; they may threaten to go live with the other parent when matters get tense. Both parents may contend from time to time for custody of a child. Children may be carriers of these tensions as well.

After it is clearly established who has primary custody and who has visiting privileges, routines need to be established. Children need to be reassured that no matter how much or how little they are in a home, they belong and there is a place for them and for any items they may want to leave behind.

Studies reveal that it is most healthy for a child to have some contact with both biological parents. Such arrangements are worth the effort but they do exact their cost on the child. One boy said, "I love to go see my dad, but I feel so sad when it's time to leave." The stress of coming and going may reveal itself in the child's behavior as he or she "gets over" a visit and works into the routine of the new family. There are, however, some rewards for families who do this multiple parenting well. As one teenage girl said to her mother, "Mom, I have a lot of people loving me."

Not only are many other people involved but laws and courts also make decisions for the remarried family. Sometimes they do this ambiguously and with uneven justice. Divorce is an adversary system carried out by the courts of our land. While the legal intent is that the settlement after a divorce (in regard to property, children, and future income) be fair and just, there is no widespread agreement as to what is "fair."

Whatever the settlement about custody, child-support payments, and so forth, it remains. Never mind that inflation increases the cost of living and that the expense of childrearing increases as children grow older. Unless the former spouses voluntarily change the settlement, it continues until the court says otherwise.

And so from time to time, one partner of the formerly married couple may again bring their affairs to the attention of the court. One may attempt to have the other parent declared incompetent and may request custody. A parent may petition for larger child-support payments. Not only the two persons but their attorneys and an impersonal court system may be part of the decision-making apparatus.

A real need of many divorced people (remarried or not) is for some mediation process to help them make realistic, fair, decisions on such matters without going to court repeatedly.

There are still further complications. Stepparents are not afforded legal rights in these family matters. A stepparent who has cared for a child for years has no right to custody of that child if one's spouse, the biological parent, dies. The law seems to see the stepparent as a stranger. The only way this can be changed is by adoption, which is not always feasible. There are separate rules in the statutes dealing with adoption by stepparents.

Stepparents also do not have specific rights in the provision of medical care for the child. Unless there is an explicit document giving a stepparent the right to authorize medical care, even emergency treatment may be delayed until the biological parent can be located.

In one western state there was a recent ruling by the department of social services stating that the resources of a stepparent shall be considered in the assessment of a fee that parents contribute toward a child's foster care, should a child need to be cared for other than in the parent's home. It would appear from this that this state's legal system exerts responsibility on stepparents without reciprocal rights. It is possible that this legal attitude would cause major difficulties in a stepfamily.

The school system is another institution of society that all too often seems not to be supportive of stepfamilies. Many schools do not have registration forms that encompass the needs of stepfamilies. The children may receive many cues that nuclear families are the norm, and that others, by implication, are second class. Some parents have the impression that the educational system may label children from stepfamilies as problems simply because they come from stepfamilies. Stepparents tell us that legal and educational systems do not contribute to the strength of families but rather often undermine it.

Children in the Remarried Family

So far we have been looking at the experience of the new remarried family through the conceptual glasses of family structure. Now we will look at the children of remarriage, what they experience, and what they need. And we will explore the tasks of the remarried couple in establishing the remarried family with children.

A first task of a couple contemplating remarriage is to inform the children of their planned marriage, to prepare the children for this marriage and the new family, and to help the children come to grips with their feelings about it and find their places within it.

It has been shown that the manner of induction, the way in which children are informed and introduced to the prospect of the remarriage, has a good bit to do with their acceptance of the marriage. The elements needed seem to be these: giving the children straightforward information; letting the children hear it directly from the adults involved before they hear it from anyone else; discussing openly all the questions the children may have about what the marriage will mean to each child personally; and providing time to get ready for the change.

A few remarrying adults tell us that they asked their children's permission to remarry. This does not seem to be a good idea. It adds a heavy responsibility and much stress to the child's life. Besides, particularly difficult problems arise if the child says no.

A couple who enjoy each other very much may be shocked to discover that their children do not share their enthusiasm. As a matter of fact, with rare exception, most remarrying couples will experience a certain amount of resistance from their children, resistance that may continue into the first few years of marriage. This resistance has many sources. The child may be contending with any or all of the following feelings:

1. "I've been dreaming and hoping that Mom and Dad would remarry and we'd all be back together again. I guess it won't happen now." (The child may go on and try to sabotage the new marriage of a parent in the hopes of reuniting parents.)

2. "It was my badness that caused my parents to break up. Now I'll never get a chance to fix it." One ten-year-old child, when her mother tried to explain the divorce to her, burst out crying, saying, "I should never have asked for that pair of shoes. Then you and Dad wouldn't have fought about money."

3. "I'm loyal to my mother and father. It would be disloyal to them to love my stepmother or stepfather."

4. "I really enjoyed just having Mom/Dad to myself in our single-parent family. We were so close. Now this new adult is going to take my place as the one Mom/Dad depends on and is closest to."

5. "My life keeps getting changed by people making big decisions that affect my life. My life feels out of control."

6. "I'm still grieving the loss of my original family. Please don't make me get used to anything more."

Of course the child may not even be aware of these feelings, which may be deep and strong but which must be dealt with by patience, discussion, time, and perhaps counseling by a good child therapist who can aid the child in expressing the things he or she cannot say.

There are, of course, exceptions to this. We are aware of children who long for another parental figure and who welcome the new marriage rather eagerly. We are aware also of a few marriages in which the courtship was carried on with the whole single-parent family; one person in the couple "married" the other person's whole family, and the whole family welcomed the new spouse/parent. It is our impression that most frequently, however, two adults discover each other, form that loving-marrying relationship and then find that they must bring their families into this decision.

Both adults and children need to work out their feelings about each other. A child can be helped to work out his or her feelings if the parental adults (biological and step-) are accepting of each other's presence and place in the life of a child. A child will have a difficult time working out these feelings if the adults are still conflicted and are unconsciously forcing the child to carry the stresses and strains that exist between them. Fortunate is the child whose biological parent gives the child permission to care about the child's stepparent.

But stepparents have some feelings with which to deal, also. In the romantic glow of courtship and the anticipated wedding, many a person has told a future mate, "I love you; I will love your children and they will love me. It will be easy, simple, and natural." Stepparents discover that this is very frequently an unrealistic expectation, at least at first. What is more accurate is that the new stepparent and the stepchildren have a person they both love—spouse to the one, parent to the other. They have compelling reasons to want to build a good life together, but it will not be automatic or easy. Stepparents who don't feel a lot of love for stepchildren sometimes berate themselves and worry about what's wrong with them. They need to be helped to understand that while the feelings of love and tenderness may be a long time coming, they can express appropriate caring behavior far ahead of their feelings. Good care, patience, fulfillment of the child's needs—these can all be provided while both child and stepparent are experiencing life together and working on deeper feelings for each other.

A part of establishing new family relationships is working out what family members will call each other, how they will introduce each other.

Younger children will probably simply be told what to call a stepparent but older children might have called their mother's male friend, "George" or "Uncle George" or "Mr. Edwards," and they may want to continue to do so for a time. If they are struggling with the issue of loyalty to their biological parent (whether that parent is dead or divorced), they may resist calling their mother's new husband "Dad" for quite some time. Our judgment is that adults should never violate a child's emotional space by insisting that a child call a stepparent "Mom" or "Dad." (Some stepparents may not be ready to be called by these titles for a while, particularly those who were childless.) Occasionally adults worry that children may not have the proper respect if they call a stepparent by his or her first name. In our opinion, the use of informal first names need not interfere with creating bonds of respect and discipline.

Children may discover ways to work this out for themselves. Carole notes that her children call both their biological father and stepfather "Dad" unless they are around their biological father. Then they call their stepfather "Henry." This seems to be out of sensitivity to their biological father's feelings and feels fine to all concerned.

Some children may want to have their stepfather's last name or may want to create a hyphenated name, using the names of their biological parent and their stepparent. In some states names can be changed without adoption (although legal procedures and fees may be involved). The combined name can allow a child to maintain bonds with a biological parent and a sense of belonging with a stepparent.

The question of names and titles probably needs to be discussed explicitly by the new remarried family. But the decision should be left open-ended because families are constantly evolving and names and titles indicating a closer deeper commitment to one another may be appropriate in time.

Very early, and continuing throughout the remarried family's life, the couple will need to deal with the question of discipline. Who should administer discipline? When? How? What are the behavioral norms for this family? How are they determined? Negotiated? Changed? Who has the right to formulate them? To enforce them?

Lucile Duberman, who studied a number of stepfamilies, felt that children in these families received the weakest parental support in the areas of discipline, advice, and socialization. She observed that when a child went for short visits to the noncustodial parent (and possibly stepparent, if the parent had remarried) the adult(s) looked upon the time as an opportunity for recreation, love, and strengthening the relationship, not for discipline. Further, when the child was at home with parent and stepparent, the stepparent hesitated to enter into disciplining even when the adult felt that the spouse was too lenient and was not disciplining the child sufficiently.[4]

Yet another observer speaks of the "eggshell phenomenon"; that is, the stepparent is so fearful of disciplining the child (fearful of the reaction of the mate) that he or she "walks on eggshells" to avoid disciplining the child. Some stepparents even fear that if they cannot get along with their children all of the time, that spouse might leave them.[5]

Many variables enter into decisions about involving the new spouse/ stepparent in the discipline process and leadership of the family. Some of the elements are:

—the similarity/dissimilarity of the two adults in regard to child-rearing philosophy and style;
—the readiness of the former single-parent family to admit a new influential member;
—the readiness of the stepparent to assume a parenting role;
—the readiness of the biological parent to share a parenting role;
—the feelings of the children about the new stepparent.

Most persons who have survived the vagueness of the discipline issue point out that this, too, is a matter that must evolve over time. The parent and stepparent do not start on a near-equal basis. Until a friend-ship relationship has been established, the child has little investment in responding to discipline. Some say that reaching this point may take eighteen to twenty-four months.

Many styles of discipline and of sharing discipline can be appropriate to the remarried family: each parent can be responsible for disciplinary decisions regarding one's own children with the stepparent as consultant and coenforcer; all decisions can be discussed and shared; each adult can have responsibility for enforcing self-selected areas of discipline important to him or her. The task of evolving a style of family leadership/ discipline in which all feel accepted and comfortable will be one of the most important tasks of the early years of remarried-family life.

Of course, this process is even more complex if either or both parents are "hybrid parents," both parents and stepparents of children who have their primary residence with them. Then, particularly if the spouses have children of similar ages, early discussion to assure equal treatment and discipline of each child and to clarify each parental role in child-rearing and discipline will need to be conducted.

The remarrying couple needs to relate their family life cycle to the life cycle of their children. The ages of the children at the time of the remarriage influence the couple's strategy for developing cooperative parenting, discipline, and family life together.

Preschool children will have less history and less memory of the previous marriage and so will probably enter into a new family most easily. The feelings of the adults strongly influence young children. At this age children have a need for routine, order, and predictability.

Routines of visiting the noncustodial parent should be clearly and simply stated, perhaps with visual helps, such as a calendar.

Children six to twelve years of age have other needs. They may have vivid memories of the breakup. They may have great need to mourn the loss of the nuclear family (whether from death or divorce) and to mourn the loss of the single-parent family. Mixed loyalties may be quite a problem. They may have problems with their own anger but may be terrified when a parent is angry with them, for fear that it signals yet another breakup.

Anger from a stepparent may also be very threatening to a child. A child may act out in ways similar to the ways he or she acted out immediately preceding the divorce. This may be the child's way of testing the stepparent before being able to trust him or her. Predictablity, reliability, promise keeping, and routine are important. Giving the child control of as much of his or her life as possible may help the child to regain a little sense that life is no longer out of control. Acceptance of the turbulence of feelings that they may be experiencing and the discovery of nondestructive ways for them to express those feelings may be much needed.

Teenage children have the life task of terminating their roles as children in the family and moving into their roles as adults. As Clifford Sager and his associates have pointed out, in the nuclear family the adolescent has a single termination process and a single beginning process with the same parents and siblings. In the remarried family, however, it is different. "There is a double termination process—the loss of the role as the child and the loss of the nuclear family. There is also a double beginning process-the beginning of the adult role in the family and the beginning as a new member in the Rem [remarried] family."[6]

It is quite possible, then, that the teenage child may not join into a remarried family completely but may turn more to peers for advice, counsel, and support. Remarrying adults with teenage children will need to be quite clear between themselves as to how they will deal with this quite understandable teenage behavior. They may need to agree on the nonnegotiable items they expect of the teenager. They may need to locate discipline with the biological parent whenever possible. Perhaps they will want to give the teenage child freedom to withdraw from much active participation in the household, leaving the door open for more active participation in the future.

The life stages of the children will influence their needs and the parental style of relating to them and involving them in family life.

The remarrying couple needs to be aware that the sexual atmosphere in the stepfamily is different from that in the nuclear family. Observers have noted that the "incest taboo" (society's clear prohibition of sex between family members) is weaker in stepfamilies. This is particularly true when stepfamilies bring together adolescents or preadolescents who did not grow up together as younger children.

At the same time, they note that there is frequently a more intense erotic atmosphere in the stepfamily. The husband and wife are, after all, newlyweds who may be very attracted to each other sexually and quite expressive of this fact. For this reason, in the remarried family there are apt to be more sexual feelings and expressions—teasing, flirting, fondling, and sexual innuendos.

One of the tasks of the remarried family will be to create such atmosphere, decorum, guidelines, and supervision that sexual expression remains within bounds that do not disrupt the new family's life together.

Long-Term Issues in the Remarried Family

So far we have spoken of issues that a remarried family faces in its early life. Having dealt with those, there will be some matters that will come up throughout the life of the remarried family that also need to be faced. We mention a few of them briefly.

Special Occasions for Children

Special occasions may include birthdays, holidays, gifts, graduations, times of achievement (plays, athletic events, music performances, and so on). As Sager and associates have noted, in nuclear families "family milestones" (such as we are discussing here) are usually times that make a family feel close. For the remarried family they may be times that "heighten feelings of loss, sorrow, and divided loyalty."[7] The two families in which the child holds membership will need to grow in maturity and sensitivity so that such days can become rich times of celebration, unmarred by family tension.

The Wedding of a Child or Stepchild

A wedding is another occasion that underlines the fact that remarriage is an unfinished institution. We have many wedding traditions, and all of them assume that the bride and groom come from intact families. For the wedding of a child of parents one or both of whom have remarried, whose names go on the invitations? Who contributes to what expenses for the wedding? Where do parents and parents' spouses sit at the wedding reception? Which family members stand in the receiving line? Who escorts the bride down the aisle if she desires parental escort? And above all, what can these families, who care about the newly marrying couple, do to make the day worry free for them and enhance their happiness on their wedding day?

These are no simple matters. Esther Wald tells of a family who came to her for therapy. The precipitating event was a wedding. Though the couple had been married for seven years, the husband's son (the groom-to-be) had planned a seating arrangement that clearly assigned his stepmother second-class status and seemed to express his hope that his divorced and remarried parents would still get back together.[8] We can imagine that the tension in the air on the day of that wedding was not at all conducive to making the wedding day a time of family reunion and celebration or to giving the young couple a happy launch! Sensitive pastors may be able to help young couples who come from remarried families plan their weddings with sensitivity for all.

Births and Dedications, Christenings, Baptisms of Grandchildren

It is very helpful if remarried couples can establish good enough relationships with ex-spouses and their spouses that they can gather with acceptance at time when children might want both parents present. The celebration of the birth of a grandchild would be one of those occasions.

Other Occasions—Joyous, Troublesome, or Sad

From our observation of remarried couples, here are some other situations that the remarried families may have to face: serious illness of a child, death of a child, delinquency or other difficulty of a child, changing financial circumstances (not only inflation but also children's growing needs—perhaps mutual decision making about college for a child) needs of aging parents, death and burial (particularly when the remarrying couple are widowed and may have started family burial plots). None of these are insurmountable long-term issues, but they can be better managed if anticipated in advance and then faced with frankness, honesty, and sensitivity.

In summary, the newly remarried family faces very difficult tasks:

—creating a new family structure with few supports or guidelines from society at large;

—building a unique family style with their children, which includes naming, disciplining, and celebrating together;

—providing for each child's needs for growth, development, and learning appropriate to that child's life stage;

—establishing rapport and trust with persons in the suprasystem so that long-term issues can be managed.

Pastoral Care for the Remarried Family

First of all, the clergyperson can offer the family the gift of pastoral concern and awareness. Sensitized to what remarried families may be experiencing in the early years, he or she can ask, and help the family to ask for itself, "What's going on in this household? How far has this family come in accomplishing the tasks of building the stepfamily structure?" This process involves such tasks as:

—bringing two former family systems together;

—clarifying the roles and expectations that the unfinished institution of remarriage forces on the family;

—recognizing and combining the diverse family heritages that have come together (One family discovered a unique way to do this. Shortly after the remarriage wedding, the stepfamily sat down and made a scrapbook. Half of it described the family the wife came from—who the children were, when they were born, what memories they treasured, what customs and holiday observances they enjoyed, and so forth; the second half of the scrapbook did the same for the husband's family. Then they included a page that contained pictures and recollections of the wedding and the new family unit. They agreed that they would collect things all year and that each New Year's they would sit down to make a scrapbook of the events of *this* family for the past year);

—providing housing space and territoriality;

—contacting the wider family structure, the other families in which the children hold membership;

—planning the arrivals and departures of children;

—dealing with the courts;

—determining what they call each other;

—handling family leadership and discipline issues;

—dealing with sexuality matters such as privacy, decorum, etc.

There is one clue that may emerge before others to indicate that a family is having difficulty. Family therapists speak of "the identified patient," the person in an upset family who may be designated as "the problem," the one who may show the signs of strain first.[9] Quite often in remarried families the "identified patient" may be a child.

Sager and associates noted that in their treatment of 213 remarried families during an eighteen-month period, 91 percent of the children expressed some problem. (That does not mean 91 percent of all children of remarried families, but of those who came to their clinic.)

The eight problems they identified were:[10]

1. Dysfunctional relationship with parents
   [custodial, noncustodial, or step-]   83%
2. Impulse control problems (including substance abuse)   38%
3. School problems   36%
4. Depressed state   29%
5. Pseudo-independence/maturity   23%
6. Extruded child (psychologically and/or physically,
   including battered child)   23%
7. Disturbance in peer relationships   21%
8. Psychosomatic complaints   12%

Another therapist, Dr. Walton Kirk, analyzes his work with children of stepfamilies. He notes that the majority range in age from twelve to fifteen, that 80 percent are male, and that 100 percent have school problems, usually performance below their ability. He notes, "A finding that even surprised me is that 80% presented a picture of passive-aggressive personality or passive-resistant behavior. The parental refrain is 'He won't do anything we tell him to—nothing we try seems to help—he just won't do anything in school.' "[11]

These family therapists suggest to us, then, that if a troubled child is the "identified patient," this may be a clear clue to the fact that not only the child but the whole family needs help. Sager's and Kirk's observations give us some clues as to what sorts of behavior and problems we should be aware of. Then perhaps we can see such behavior as a call for help and offer to the family early detection and intervention for the problems they may be experiencing.

The concerned and aware cleryperson might learn from therapists a model for offering care to the remarried family. Sager and associates point out that when a remarried family presents itself to their agency for treatment, they have several goals for the initial evaluation period.[12]

1. To establish rapport and a working relationship with each member of the remarried family

2. To learn from each member what that member perceives the problems to be
3. To begin to establish treatment goals with each family member
   a. for the family member himself or herself
   b. for the family of which that person is a part
   c. for the whole remarried-family system (including all persons involved in some way)
4. To develop a preliminary hypothesis as to the dysfunction in this family and to develop a responsive treatment plan

Sager and his associates see therapy beginning with the first telephone call. It is their intention to draw together as many members of the current remarried suprasystem as possible for at least one meeting to discuss matters relating to the welfare of children. Then the therapist may plan for counseling of individuals and of smaller subsystems (which could include children; children and the residential biological parent and the stepparent; children and the other biological parent, whom they occasionally visit alone, with his or her present spouse; children and grandparents, and so forth).

Such a treatment model might readily adapt to a pastoral care model. That is, a clergy might ponder, "What is the suprasystem in this remarried family? Who is involved? What are the subsystems? How are they doing? Are there people involved in these systems who might need pastoral contact and care but who are out of my realm of contact? If so, can I perhaps contact their clergyperson and suggest that as colleagues we each offer support to different parts of this remarried family suprasystem, helping all to adjust successfully to their new status and to each other?"

There may be times when a clergyperson would initiate the calling together of all adults whose lives touch the children of remarriage, if it seems advisable. A fairly frequent set of problems in remarriage has to do with children, custody, visits, and so forth. If the clergy senses that there are problems here that could get worse, then she or he might be advised to urge a meeting of children and any parents, stepparents, grandparents, or others who might be involved in the children's care and welfare. Such a gathering might be quite tense, but the clergy should take charge and not allow this to be a time when persons attack each other personally. Rather, a calm discussion of matters touching the welfare, happiness, and growth of the children should be conducted. Children should have a chance to speak about what makes it easy and what makes it difficult to transfer from one house to the other, to be in touch with all these parental adults. Specific suggestions can be developed with a possible future meeting planned to test how these arrangements are working out. The clergyperson can suggest this if she or he has remained caring pastor to both parties during the divorce. In carrying out a difficult but important meeting such as this, one should not allow oneself to be trapped into taking sides or into allowing verbal abuse to take place. Such a gathering can have the important consequence of showing that the people involved can deal with one another fairly and calmly and that they are allies in the efforts of the children's welfare.

As the remarriage evolves, the clergy may be able to help family members deal with the vagueness and the ambiguity they may feel in their family life. Sager suggests that a valuable technique for this is contracting. Just as the couple need to work out their contract with each other, they need to work out a contract with the children. Sager suggests the following contract as a discussion device with older children (ages ten to seventeen) who live with a parent who has remarried. The therapist begins by asking questions about what parent the child lives with, and what stepparents, siblings, and stepsiblings are in the remarried family. Then, the following questions are addressed to the child/youth. It is suggested that the child/youth write out the answers so that they may be used for future family-therapy discussions.

1. What kind of family would you like to have? Describe it.
2. What kind of family member would you like to be in such a family?
3. What kind of stepparent would you like to have? What kind of stepchild would you like to be?
4. What about stepbrothers and stepsisters? What would you like for them, and what would you like to be to them?
5. How would you like the mother or father with whom you live to act? How would you like to act in return?
6. How would you like the father or mother whom you visit to act? What would you like to give in return?
7. What would you like to see changed (if anything)?
8. In your opinion, how does your parent's remarriage affect your life? Is your life better or worse? What advantages and what disadvantages are there for you in your parent's remarriage?

9. Where are you more comfortable—in your mother's house or in your father's house? Specifically, why?

10. Draw a picture of those who are in the family that you think of as *your* family. Label who each one is. Include yourself.[13]

Helping children to write out the answers to such questions, discussing related topics with other family members, helping each to hear and respond to the needs and hopes of the others, and then helping the family members to explore their style and roles would be to facilitate a most constructive healing experience indeed.

Using many resources, the clergy can support the remarried family and help them to see that building a strong, caring family life together is within their Christian calling. The Bible urges parents not to provoke children to anger but to bring them up with gentle discipline; this is not based on any biological parenting relationship but upon the dignity of the child and the worth of the child's soul in the sight of God, which holds true whether the family is a nuclear family or a stepfamily. When the Bible urges a quality of loving that is filled with unconquerable good will, it is not referring to automatic, biological-family love. We are motivated to love by God's love for us, a resource available to remarried families as well as original ones.

The Bible describes the Christian church as a group of people who previously had nothing in common but who came together because each shared a common love for Jesus Christ, and that description of the church comes very close to describing what a remarried family is. Often remarried families come together because the one thing they have in common is love for one family member; perhaps this person is the woman who is mother to some family members and wife to another. And, indeed, the church is called the "family" or "household" of God.

The Bible speaks of being "adopted" into God's family through Jesus Christ, and the Bible makes clear that this adoption is a glorious privilege. Remarried families who are working to "adopt" each other may have a clearer grasp of what the Bible is saying than those who have never had such an experience.

Building the remarried family, difficult though it may be, is a task that has all the dignity of Christian calling and Christian service. There are times when the clergyperson may share this insight with those in the midst of establishing such families. At those times, it may be good news indeed.

Building a Caring Church for Widowed, Divorced, and Remarried People—And Dealing with the Issues That Emerge

So far we have been addressing the issue of what the clergy can do personally to be caring, supportive, and pastoral with persons in remarriage relationships. But both the clergy and the remarried persons exist in a larger context—faith community, secular community, society, culture. The clergyperson would be ill-advised to ignore this larger context and attempt to "go it alone" in caring for remarried persons. The clergy would do better to attempt to draw the church community into this caring process. Quite likely, this will not be an easy task.

For theological reasons, cultural reasons, and personal reasons, people in the church community may find it quite difficult to reach out to the divorced and the remarried. (Some have less problems with the widowed, but it should not be assumed that total sensitivity exists for widowed persons either.) Such problems should not be ignored but faced. Then, perhaps, the church can at least experience growth and progress, even if it does not give unanimous support, in developing a sense of caring for persons of different marriage and parenting styles.

We feel that in approaching this subject we need first to talk about the total church's ministry with divorcing, divorced, and widowed persons and with single parents. If the church has not been sensitive to these persons, it may have lost the opportunity to minister to remarried families that will be formed when some of these widowed, divorced, unmarried persons later remarry.

So we ask what the caring church, concerned individuals, and a supportive pastor can do. And then we ask what the clergy can do to bring this style of congregational life into being.

What Can the Caring Church, Concerned Individuals Within That Church, and a Supportive Pastor Do?

What can the church do to aid persons in the healthy recovery from the grief of death or divorce and the loss of a first marriage?

The church can acknowledge that divorce happens to members of its congregation. It can stop being so secretive. Almost all churches (at least middle-sized and small churches) have a time in the worship service when they share news of church family members. Have you ever noticed how selective that information is? Physical illnesses are mentioned but not nervous breakdowns. Deaths are mentioned but rarely divorces. While of course persons' privacy should be protected if they don't want their news shared, still it is true that divorce is a rather public event. Isn't it true also that an important step for the divorcing persons and those who care about them is to make the information known that a divorce is taking place? Perhaps other churches might follow the lead of one church of which we learned. During this church's news-sharing time, persons experiencing a separation or divorce are given an opportunity to share that information with the congregation so that the congregation might be concerned about the welfare of each family member.

The church can see to it that support groups and support systems are provided for persons undergoing these experiences. Various people— widows, persons in the trauma of the early stages of divorce, long-term single persons, and so on—have different needs. An individual church may seek to create and provide support groups for these persons, or it might cooperate with other churches to do so. It also might become informed about support systems provided in the community and, at the very least, refer persons there. Church members who participate in such community-based support groups may take other persons from the church to those groups. Perhaps they can form a subsystem within the community support group, offering the double support of sharing the same life circumstance and sharing the same church. (The next chapter will provide resource suggestions as to how a church can offer its own support groups and/or discover what groups may exist in the community or larger area. These resources will help a church to implement the suggestions offered in this chapter.)

The clergyperson may offer to serve as a resource to those agencies. Social workers and therapists may have had no training in theology. Sometimes these persons even view the church as a hindrance to the growth of clients, due to their stereotypical understanding of traditional theology. The pastor may need aid from agencies that provide counseling services to support groups, but the pastor may also have something valuable to offer to them.[1]

Not only can the church make sure that the divorcing couple have the support they need, it can also help a divorcing couple learn what divorce really is. Divorce is a process, not a single event. Divorce is the restructuring of a relationship, not the end of it. Particularly when there are children about which both parents care and for which both parents assume some responsibility, divorce will be a continuing restructured relationship.

It is hoped that in time a couple will reach the point at which they achieve an "emotional divorce." That is, neither partner has the need to hurt the other. Nor does either partner secretly cherish hopes of a reconciliation, which neither the other partner nor circumstances permit. Rather, with a degree of objectivity, the couple achieve freedom from the painful bonds of each other. They can deal with each other objectively and fairly about the issues that still mutually concern them. They can provide a healthy nondestructive atmosphere for their children and can help the children make the transition from one home to the other rather smoothly.

Support groups (particularly those that are well informed about the pattern of adjustment growth in divorced persons) can be one aid to achieving realistic emotional divorces. The divorce ceremony, mentioned in chapter 2, might be another way. Still another way involves providing much personal care, support, and friendship for the divorcing individual. The divorcing individual may be traumatized for a long time and may need to spend hours talking about anger, loneliness, or depression. A caring and patient support person is needed, perhaps one who has been through the same experience.

When ministering to the widowed person, the church needs to take a careful look at what that person needs. After the bereavement gifts of flowers and food are gone, after the services and receptions are over, after relatives who came to lend support have gone home, the person will have needs of which the church should be aware.

Coping with loneliness, income-tax forms, and legal arrangements; filling the need for new groups and new ways of relating; finding persons to do the housework or yard work that the deceased spouse used to do; making decisions about the deceased spouse's clothing and other artifacts of living—all these and more remain to be done. Wise is the church that has individuals and groups that provide support to persons in such circumstances.

The church—both in the church's library and in the pastor's counseling library—can make available important literature on the subject of the divorce process and the grief process. One counselor, himself a divorced person, told us, "When I was going through my divorce, I was an avid reader, not only about divorce and surviving it, but also about things that would help me deal with my rather battered self-esteem. Likewise, in my counselees, I discover an openness, an urgency to read, learn, and discover—at least in some of them.''

The church can be sensitive to the spiritual pilgrimages and spiritual struggles of widowed and divorcing persons. Both may feel a sense of radical aloneness, guilt, regret, and a questioning of their relationship with God. Persons who have long been active in the church may wonder if they belong there any more. They may conclude that they do not and may drop out, temporarily or for good. Persons who had not been a part of a church community may sense a need for human support and divine support and may come back.

Church persons need to be aware that death or divorce have a drastic impact on all of a person's life, including one's spiritual life. Caring church people should not be afraid to ask, "What's happening in your spiritual life, and what can we do to be of help?"

We now come to the most difficult item of all, what a church must do if it is to be able to act on any of the other suggestions with enthusiasm and with effectiveness. The church needs to address its own attitudes about divorce.

Earlier in this book, we offered a pastoral theology of divorce and remarriage in an attempt to help clergy who have not yet worked through their attitudes about these matters. After the minister has worked through his or her attitudes, it will be necessary to help the church to do the same thing. It is hoped that chapter 1 of this book and the additional resources to which we refer will provide the clergy with the necessary tools to do this. When David Dalke surveyed ministers on this topic, one of the questions he asked was "What is your personal stand in regard to divorce?" Nearly one-half of the two hundred responses he received used punitive words in their answers. Such words as "cop-out, tragic failure, sin (not 'missing the mark' but rather 'against God and another human') and contrary to the will of God" were among the responses.[2]

In a recent discussion of ministry with the divorced, a pastor suggested, "I can accept these people, but I cannot condone what they have done." That sounds like judgmentalism. Said a laywoman in the same discussion, "When a divorce takes place in my church, I try to decide who is at fault and who is the victim. Then I try to give the victim lots of support, but I avoid the one at fault." Judgment again.

One counselor with whom we visited noted that divorcing couples with whom she worked frequently felt that there was no longer a place for them in their churches. Somehow they felt unwanted, forced out. In the perception of these couples, the minister was not a strong support for helping them to stay within the church. They sensed that she or he either was neutral on the subject or didn't want to meet the resistance. Whether or not this is an accurate observation of the facts, these persons felt the church withdrawing from them at a very troubling time in their lives.

Another pastor noted that his congregation had real difficulties when divorces occurred within that congregation. He pointed out that this was not based on biblical reasons but on other values and personal-need issues. From listening carefully to the anguish of congregation members when divorces took place, he concluded that there were three reactions among his church members. (a) Some members expressed anger that the divorcing individuals were putting their own happiness ahead of the institution of marriage. Such persons had marriages that had not been overly happy, but they understood that their duty was to "tough it out," enduring the difficult marriage because they considered the institution of marriage sacred and enduring; (b) other members expressed envy, seeing the divorcing persons as courageous and strong and themselves as weak and indecisive since they dared not do the same thing; (c) still others—particularly wives who did not have means of earning a living independently—expressed terror that the same thing could happen to them.

Other persons condemn divorce as the sign of a decadent society. They note that our society does not prepare persons for the discipline of marriage and this makes it easy to marry and easy to divorce. They conclude that persons enter both marriage and divorce too lightly and that these irresponsible decisions are damaging not only to children but also to society at large. Such observations may have some merit to them, but it doesn't follow that persons should use divorcing people as scapegoats for their anger over an imperfect marital system and an imperfect society.

Some church members would readily grant the right of divorce to victims of desertion, abuse, and adultery, but would be less decisive about others. A naive, unreflective reading of some of Jesus' teachings (reading that ignores the context) seems to feed and reinforce such attitudes. (We attempted to analyze those teachings carefully, in context, in chapter 1 and so will not repeat that analysis here.)

Some worry that the church's acceptance and sensitivity to divorcing people may contribute to further decline in the stability of existing marriages. The answer to this concern must be that the present condition came into being without the blessing of the church. It is unlikely that a loving, accepting church is going to cause a larger stampede of divorces. (At the same time, we share our bias that in some cases the mistake was the marriage, or the conduct of the marriage, and that some divorces should take place.)

Many forces seem to converge, then, to make the church's attitude toward divorce rigid and condemnatory. But we believe that there are many more forces that can impact the church to make it a gracious, loving, nonjudgmental place for people who are divorcing. Some of these forces are:

—basic human compassion;

—the presence in the church of some people who have been through the hurt and pain of widowhood and divorce;

—a more aware and accurate reading of Jesus' teaching on this subject;

—pastoral encouragement for persons to look at their own anger, envy, and fears when divorce takes place; and pastoral help so that they will recognize that these feelings are not good bases on which to make decisions;

—the influence of the life, cross, and teachings of Jesus—including his words "Judge not . . . " (Matthew 7:1); " . . . love one another; even as I have loved you . . . " (John 13:34); "Let the one who is without sin among you be the first to throw a stone . . . "(John 8:7); "Neither do I condemn you; go, and do not sin again" (John 8:11)— on attitudes toward the whole of human experience and failure;

—the firm, courageous, theologically based leadership of pastors who are convinced that compassionate caring by the church for divorced/widowed persons is one expression of the gospel.

Robert Elliott has put it well:

Marriage is *alive* when it nurtures the personhood and authentic life of the partners, it is *dead* when it ceases to do that, and it is *deadly* when it becomes injurious and destructive to the personhood of either or both partners. When a relationship comes to the point, however, where it is marked more by death than by life, more by hurt then by healing, and when genuine efforts to renew and revitalize it have failed, it is important that permission be given to bring that relationship to as dignified and honorable an end as possible. It is here that theology of divorce needs to be articulated.[3]

Somehow congregations need to discover that the pain and anguish they feel when they learn of a marital breakup is but a small part of the pain and anguish that both members of the separating couple are feeling. The congregation can and must learn to support them and to suffer with them.

What can the church do to provide care and support to single parents and single-parent families?

A single-parent advocate put it to me this way: "After the sorrow of the death or divorce, after the courts, after the emotional struggle of admitting the loss—after all that, single parenthood is what is left. And it stays with you for a long time!"

And so, in addition to all that has been mentioned, there are some other things a church can do in regard to single parents and single-parent families.

Again, admit they're there, both in the community (in great numbers) and in the church (probably in fewer numbers). It has been noted that while most Americans still think of "typical" family as the intact marriage in which the husband is the breadwinner and there are one or more children at home, presently only 7 percent of all American families fit into that category. The other family types would include two-career marriages with or without children, childless or empty-nest marriages, remarried families, and single-parent families. We do not have the exact percentages for these, but it is known that 21 percent of all parents in America are single parents! (Of course that percentage will vary from community to community.) If we are seeing a tiny minority of single parents in our congregations, then either we are not ministering to the needs of single parents or they do not think there is a ministry in our church for them. However it comes out, we have a problem and an opportunity.

The church can accept single parenthood as a viable life-style. When a single-parent advocate was interviewing ministers in my community, she asked one clergy what was the most important service he felt he should offer to single parents. The minister quickly responded, "Get them married as soon as possible." In my opinion and in the opinion of the interviewer, this represents a destructive attitude. It does not contribute to the dignity of single parenthood, which some people choose and some have thrust upon them. It does not contribute to effective long-term marriages made from strength and free choice.

Before church people are ready to accept single parenthood as a viable life-style, they may have to correct some misunderstandings:

Misunderstanding: "The broken home (divorce, single parenthood) is a major cause of juvenile deliquency."

Fact: In a study of approximately 18,000 delinquent children, only one-tenth of the delinquent boys and about one-fifth of the delinquent girls came from homes broken by divorce or separation.[4]

Misunderstanding: It is always a destructive experience for a child to live in a home broken by divorce or death.

Fact: The evidence is that it is the emotional situation at home rather than the actual parental division which affects a child's adjustment. In severely conflicted homes, it may be to the child's great advantage if the parents separate. "The truth is children have a better chance of meaningful adjustment to life's changes and challenges outside a hurtful family situation, than in one."[5]

E. E. Lemasters, a professor of social work writes, "The one parent family has not been proven to be psychologically disfunctional—its main problems are socioeconomic. Our society has never properly organized for the one parent family."[6]

One single parent told me, "I would love to be a part of a church that says to me, 'We believe in you and your ability to function as a single parent. We believe you can do it. We want to support you, but this support is of the type we offer to all persons here. It is not a message of pity or paternalism or condescension. We are not saying, "You poor thing, you deficit family." '"

The church can offer community and help to single parents. One formerly single parent offered the caution, "Ask us what we need; don't assume you know." When I followed his advice and asked a few single parents what acts of community and caring would communicate to them, these are some of the answers I received:

—I'd like a hug now and then. Just because I'm divorced doesn't mean I'm contagious.

—Include single parents among those you invite to a dinner party, or when you have family get-togethers, invite my kids and me also.

—Invite us to share holidays with you. Don't assume we'd rather be alone. We may not be able to come, but it feels good to be asked.

—Perhaps the church could develop a skill bank. We could do a skill exchange; you know, we could exchange trimming hedges for some homebaked bread or something else.

—I think all single parents need to have assertiveness training. We need to be assertive about our viability as families and the needs of ourselves and our children. Even men that function well in the business world need to learn assertiveness with new settings—schools, child-care agencies, and so forth.

—When children make gifts at church school for parents, let the child make two if the child's parents live apart.

—Stay-at-home parents, whether single or married, can offer to be emergency-contact parents for children of employed parents, whether married or single.

—Offer to take my kids for a day so that I can clean house or just have the luxury of a few hours alone. Offers of babysitting are always appreciated. One can love one's kids but still need to get away from them!

—Do lots of things in the church about family life and parenting. Sensitize speakers to deal with all kinds of family life.

—Help build community. Plan potluck dinners for single parents or for all parents so that we can sense community and support.

—I'd like a few things that respond to my needs as a single parent, but I don't want to be isolated from the life of the church as a whole.

—When I was totally broke, could not pay my bills, and had no food for my little boy, one of my friends called my church and told them. They quickly and quietly appeared with a bag of groceries and some money to tide me over. They told me to let them know if I needed help again. I've never had to ask again, but I've never forgotten their willingness to help.

—Don't forget us single parents when you are looking for help. Most of us are limited in what we can do, of course, for many of us are full-time employees and full-time parents. But short-term projects are something we can help on. And we don't want just to receive. We want to help!

Recognition, acceptance, awareness, respect, sensitivity, and support—these basic human qualities are the gifts churches can offer to the single parents that may come into their midst.

What can the church do to provide effective premarriage and wedding help to persons entering remarriage?
We will not repeat what was said in chapter 3 about the minister's opportunity in planning remarriage weddings with the couple, and in chapter 2 about helping the couple be ready for remarriage. We simply want to point out that the church as well as the minister is involved in such support systems to persons entering remarriage.

The church might participate in premarriage preparation. One remarried couple told us that when they were preparing for their marriage,
they were in the care of a Quaker meeting. There is a practice in that
fellowship that when a couple is anticipating marriage, a group of
people hold a meeting on "clearness" with them. This is a group of
people from the fellowship who visit with the couple to discuss with
them their relationship, their strengths, their weaknesses, their hopes,
and so on. When the group members feel "clear," or affirmative, about
the upcoming marriage, they recommend that the couple proceed. Remarried persons were among those who counseled with the couple at
their "clearness meeting," and they felt this was particularly helpful.
They sensed the concern, interest, and support of their faith community
in the step they were taking into remarriage.

Even if churches do not share the "clearness meeting" custom,
remarried laypersons in their congregations might have some special
gifts to offer in premarriage counseling. Perhaps this could be quite
informal. A remarried couple with some similarities in previous marital
history and with children of similar ages at the time of the remarriage
might have a couple over for dinner. They might visit about the issues
they faced and the problems they resolved. The two couples might
compare notes. Thus the newly remarrying couple might gain insight
into the remarriage experience while forming a supportive relationship
for the future.

The church and the minister need to be in harmony about policy in
regard to weddings of remarried people. One pastor put it well, "Even
though I am a part of a church that grants autonomy to each believer
and even though my denomination does not have explicit rulings about
weddings, I have a clear sense that when I officiate at a wedding,
somehow my church's blessing goes along with that act. People in the
congregation sense it also. They raise questions and express discomfort
when I choose to preside at a wedding service of someone whose
behavior has made them wonder about the appropriateness of a church
wedding. And in a relatively small community, people know a lot about
other people or think they do!"

This particular pastor had an important point. Though the pastor can
give courageous leadership in helping remarrying couples experience
forgiveness/acceptance and the blessing of God on their union, the
pastor cannot move too great a distance from the stance of his or her
congregation. The historical stance of a particular church on such
subjects, the geographical location (since remarriage is more accepted

in some parts of the country than others), the size of the congregation and the community, the pronouncements of one's denomination on divorce and remarriage—all these and more will enter into a church's informal, unofficial position on such matters.

The minister needs to face and discuss such matters with the policy-making board of the congregation. And the minister will need to live with its conclusions. Otherwise, compassionate as he or she may feel toward the couple coming for support, the pastor will have to say in essence, "I am a maverick minister and will go ahead with your wedding. However, please keep it quiet, and I must tell you that there's no place for you in my church."

Church members can express support at the wedding. This may be expressed in such simple things as attendance. (Some persons agonize over attending remarried weddings, wondering if it expresses disloyalty to the former spouse. While the caring person needs to be sensitive to the feelings and needs of the former spouse, attendance at the wedding shows no such disloyalty. It simply recognizes what is and offers care and support to the persons who have arrived at this point in life.) Support may also be expressed in the gifts people give to the remarrying couple. Generally, remarrying people have households filled with items and don't need the same things as newlyweds. Many remarrying couples have the problem of owning two of everything and needing to dispose of things. A personalized gift, expressing prayers and hopes for the couple's enduring happiness is appropriate. Gifts that offer continuing support—for example, a "gift certificate" for a future dinner, outing, or excursion together—are fitting and meaningful. The support may be expressed by providing whatever help is needed to make the wedding (wherever it occurs) and the reception (however small, simple, and informal it may be) occasions that are marked by the presence, care, and support of friends.

What insensitivities or counterproductive attitudes or actions should churches seek to avoid in regard to remarried families?

Churches should educate themselves to avoid inaccurate use of names. Three or more last names may exist in the same household. In the coauthor's household, Carole *Della Pia* (her maiden name, to which she reverted after the termination of her first marriage) is married to Henry *Terry* and is the mother of Kristen, Kelly and Bob *King* (their father's name). When the church, the school, or the doctor calls her about her children, she does not want to be called "Mrs. King." "Mrs. King" is the name of her former husband's present wife, and Carole would prefer not to be called by that name. The point is that although five persons live in the same household and are becoming family together, each of the three surnames has importance. They did not choose these names to confuse other people. They choose to use them for the significance these names carry for each person. If church persons ignore this, it is as though they subtly say, "We're not really interested in who you are."

When the church uses names—in church directories, religious education class rolls, newsletters and bulletins, and so on—it should try to report the name of each family member accurately. Likewise, persons who deal with the children—church school teachers and youth group advisers, for example—should be helped to be sensitive to the life situation and names of the children and their families. It is also important that the church school teachers know what children call the adults in their lives.

The church can avoid insensitivities of time and calendar also. In its zeal to promote faithful participation, churches may put guilt trips on youngsters who cannot be "faithful." Why? Because every other weekend they are with their other parent (perhaps in another community, perhaps at another church). Church leaders should be sensitive to the reasons for a child's absences and communicate to the child that they understand. "Faithfulness" can include participation in the other parent's church or attendance on the Sundays the child is at home.

If a church school class or youth group is planning an event that a child would especially like to attend, they should try to check in advance to see whether this fits the child's family visitation schedule. (Of course, if there are several such children, this may become impossibly complicated, but it is a consideration of which to be aware.)

The church should avoid insensitivities that stepparents often endure elsewhere. Stepparents have no legal rights in regard to children and often are viewed by school authorities and others as persons who have no influence, decision-making power, or interest in the children. The church can be sensitive to the stepparent's efforts to be a "real" parent—to be involved and caring and to participate in the learning, discovery, and spiritual growth of the child. Stepparents should be involved in parent conferences and parent activities within the church.

The church should be sensitive about family membership and involvement. For instance, earlier we suggested that children in single-parent families should be allowed to make two gifts for parents if parents live apart. The child in a remarried family may need to make four gifts: two Mother's Day cards, two Father's Day cards. The child may want all parents and stepparents to come and see him or her perform in a program or be present at his or her baptism or confirmation. It is the church person's task to be sensitive and welcoming, to all the concerned adults in that child's life.

What supportive, helpful things can churches do to help strengthen remarried families?

The church can work through its own attitudes about remarriage. Earlier in this chapter we spoke of the church needing to deal with its attitudes about divorce. If it found that difficult to do, it may have even greater difficulty in dealing with remarriage, at least some remarriages. The same combination of forces converge on the topic of remarriage.

It appears to us that congregations deal with some remarriage situations fairly easily and some with difficulty. The classifications are something like this:

a. Easy-to-cope-with situation: A new family comes to the congregation. In time the family reveals that it is a remarried family.

b. Fairly-easy-to-cope-with situation: Two persons, at least one of whom is divorced, start coming to church. They request that the pastor officiate at their wedding, and they enter into the life of the congregation.

c. Fairly difficult situation: A couple within the congregation experiences a divorce. In time one of the divorced couple meets someone from outside, and eventually requests marriage by the pastor within the church.

d. Most difficult situation: (Let me propose this one as a case study. If you think it sounds familiar, let me assure you that this is a composite of at least a half dozen situations reported to me.) Two couples in the same church begin to recognize their marital disharmony at approximately the same time. Later they divorce at approximately the same time. While all four estranged spouses and their children still participate to some extent in the church, one partner from each of the former marriages come together and eventually marry.

The last example of remarriage stirs a lot of discomfort and not inconsiderable anger among church members. One person screams at his pastor, who officiated, 'Is the Bible true? Is divorce a sin as it says?" "Yes," shouts another, equally excited, "and is remarriage adultery?" The pastor's responses do not seem to satisfy them. Somehow this most difficult situation brings church members face to face with some issues they had uneasily avoided when faced with situations (a), (b), and (c).

How would you deal with this difficult case? Would you deal with it at this point? Or would you have made different decisions earlier if you had been the minister in this situation? I raised this question with a number of persons. Here are some of the answers I received.

—"This is just the sort of thing you get into when you do remarriages. I would refuse to do all remarriages and avoid this sort of destructive, tangled mess."

—"I do officiate at remarriages. But in a case like this, I'd have to balance the need of the church community over against the need of the couple, and somehow I alone can't take the blessing of my church with me into this one. I would feel somewhat inconsistent, but if the couple would ask me to officiate at their wedding, I'd say, 'I'm sorry, but no.' And if they asked me if there was a place for them in the church afterwards, I'd again say, 'I'm sorry, but no.' "

—"I agree. I'd tell the couple that while we are supportive of remarriage, we also try to be sensitive to other persons. To support this marriage is to be insensitive to the two former spouses."

—"I'd feel that my beliefs would lead me to participate in the wedding. And having done that I'd have no other choice but to 'tough it out,' hoping that time would heal wounds and people would accept the situation. Probably not all four former spouses would want to stay in the church, but I would attempt to make church available to all."

—"This is an opportunity to discover what the church as redemptive fellowship is all about. I might even go to the couple, tell them that they have become some sort of symbol of people's difficulty with remarriage, and ask them if they are willing to be a topic of study and discussion. Then I would gather a wide variety of groups in the church and talk out both the theology of remarriage and the feelings about it. One way or another, a community cannot avoid feelings that exist. The church is a microcosm of life. It needs to work out its life on this and every other troubling issue."

Before they face such difficult issues, it would be appropriate for churches to discuss these questions: "What do we believe about remarriage? What should we do about remarriage? Who makes the decisions? Are there some circumstances in which the decision maker must say no?'' It is impossible to emphasize enough how basic this step really is.

The questions that came up in response to that case study are the ones that haunt us as we seek to develop supportiveness of the church for remarried persons, so let's look at them directly.

''Is divorce sin?'' One pastor, himself divorced and remarried, told us, ''If either member of a couple coming to me has been divorced, I share with them my belief that divorce is a sin. It is a broken promise to the other person, to self, to God. Divorce, then, is a matter that must be settled not only with the state, but with one's self and with one's own faith. I often then go on to share my own experience, how I felt divine forgiveness and divine permission to go on to a new relationship.''

''Is divorce sin?'' Yes, if by sin we mean ''falling short of the mark of God's intention for human relationships and of our own ideals.'' Yes, if by sin we mean separation from God, that universal human characteristic. (And the joy of the Christian gospel is that sin is forgivable!) But, no, divorce is not sin if by sin we mean a decision that is always wrong or evil. Sometimes divorce may be a necessary step toward wholeness and healing, which, we believe, is God's will for every person.

''Is remarriage adultery?'' We have to live with that striking phrase in Jesus' teaching. Yes, in the sense that it marks the break with the ideal of a lifelong, enduring, marital relationship. No, if one uses the term ''adultery'' to mean that the committed relationships of remarried women and men are outside the blessing and guidance of God. The most basic message of the Bible is God's love. Grace prevails!

Somehow churches need to be carried along in this reflective process so that the whole congregation is ready to be a caring community that can nurture and encourage the strength of the remarried family.

The church can provide opportunity for preventative measures that contribute to the health of the remarried family. In their excellent book, *Treating the Remarried Family*, Clifford J. Sager and associates (after devoting fifteen chapters to the dynamics of the remarried family and its treatment) offer a chapter on prevention of an unhealthy remarried family in which they suggest three levels of prevention.

In primary prevention, people are offered new educational experiences that can provide added knowledge and understanding. Such experiences may cause persons to question their habitual ways of thinking, feeling, and acting and may help them to develop new methods of

dealing with themselves, their families, and their social environment.[7]
This might take place through printed material, films, television, and/
or radio. It might also take place through public forums and other
information meetings for large groups. Occasional lecture-discussions
with groups that meet regularly (service clubs, parent-teacher organizations, various groups within a church) offer one way to introduce the
topic. Long-term lecture-discussion programs might then be offered to
those who desire more specific information and insight. Sager and his
associates see this primary prevention occurring in the public media
and through school systems, medical clinics, religious institutions,
community centers, and employee assistance programs.

According to Sager, secondary prevention consists of early identifi-
cation of cases and early intervention when a nonproductive pattern
seems to be developing in a relationship. They point out the importance
of pre-remarriage counseling, since many problems of remarriage can
be anticipated and dealt with in this process. They then sadly conclude
that very few remarrying couples seek such counsel, commenting,
"Except for those who wish to be married by particular members of
the clergy whose church requires premarital instruction, there appears
to be no current way of overcoming mass resistance to premarital
education."[8] Their comment underlines the very special opportunity
for doing premarital counseling that is available to clergy prepared to
do this.

Sager suggests that there is a tertiary level of prevention, which is
rehabilitation and prevention of long-term complications of any dysfunction that may have occurred. But his book does not discuss this
level of prevention.

I have summarized this viewpoint of preventative measures to offer
a hint of how wide a range of activity might be involved for a group
of people who, from the perspective of their Christian faith, have
decided to be advocates on behalf of the remarried family. Much reeducation needs to occur within the churches, and much of it must also
occur outside if people are to become more aware of the nature of
remarried families and if remarried families are to be more self-aware
and informed about possible sources of help.

Incidentally, when doing reeducation about remarriage, church leaders may want to examine their own curricula and libraries to discover
how much of it is oriented to the intact family. Not everything can be
changed overnight, but steps can be taken to enable the teachers to
recognize varying family styles. Those who create curriculum can be

given suggestions that future curriculum be more sensitive to different family styles.

The caring church can provide a variety of ongoing support systems for remarried families. Any church, no matter how small or large, can offer some type of support to remarrying families. It might consist of one or more of the following approaches.

a. A church could facilitate one-on-one support (stepmother to stepmother, stepfather to stepfather), couple-to-couple support, or family-to-family support. Remarried persons who are aware and sensitive human beings could be asked by their church to be available as resource persons to all newly remarried persons within their church.

b. A church or a group of churches could sponsor occasional short courses (three to six sessions each) on some aspect of remarriage or stepfamilies. These could include:

—discussions of some excellent books in the field;

—talks by and dialogues with marriage-family counselors or other knowledgeable people;

—movies, dramas, and other nonthreatening activities that raise consciousness about remarriage and stepfamilies.

c. A church or churches could have a group that was primarily social, enjoying couple or family activities together. From time to time it might have a speaker or promote such short term courses as mentioned in (b).

d. A church or churches could provide an ongoing support group that would meet weekly or monthly and be available to new couples whenever they desired to attend. In addition to providing ongoing support, this group would meet to discuss the topics on people's minds or an announced topic with a leader or resource person.

All of these suggestions may sound good, but whatever plan a church develops, it may encounter a widely shared problem: even very good programs do not seem to draw very many remarried families.

When we coauthors were first becoming interested in this field, we started such a group. We offered a short-term (four-session) course. The first two sessions featured a highly respected family sociologist and a couple who are outstanding therapists. Then we developed the remaining two sessions to respond to the identified needs of the group. This course was sponsored by a group of nine churches of varying denominations, which worked closely together. After vigorous promotion we were able to get together a group of about twenty people. (Nearly a fourth of these people were professionals from agencies in the community, and they came seeking insight into working with the remarried family!)

When we evaluated what happened, we were able to make several observations. (a) The course was too short, although people told me they probably would not have committed if we had made it much longer. (b) The core of an ongoing support group could have come out of this experience. (Unfortunately, changing life circumstances meant that we never called that group into being.) (c) At least one couple came with deeper needs than could be met by such a group, and we needed to be ready with both personal counsel and referrals to professional help for that couple. (d) We had a feeling that the multiple-church sponsorship made it easier for some to come to the group. They might have feared too much intensity or exposure if only persons from one church were there. Also multiple-church sponsorship gave to persons who came a sense of a broader concern and base of support. (e) In spite of the novice status of the leaders, it was a good and enriching experience for those who participated. The evaluation indicated that much more could be done in this and other communities.

Sager and his associates note that when they examined the reasons for small attendance at educational events for remarried couples sponsored by their own and other agencies, they discovered one possible reason: the negativism in much of the advertising. They changed their strategy to suggest that the goal of the group was for participants to learn to cope positively with situations rather than merely to deal with the suffering caused by problems. They also used catch phrases to suggest how widespread and acceptable remarried families are. Here are some of them: " 'Four out of every 10 marriages involve an adult who has been married before.' 'One out of every four families includes stepchildren.' 'Eighteen million children under the age of 18 have become part of stepfamilies.' 'Each year, half a million adults become stepparents.' 'There is a new type of American family—the stepfamily.' "[9]

We conclude that when anyone originates groups or courses for remarried persons, positive, high-quality, and widespread publicity is needed. Also, there need to be many direct invitations to specific people. The planners are asking for disappointment if they just plan the group or course, announce it, and wait for people to show up. Though we are convinced that such groups may be needed and useful, there is a certain resistance to getting them started.

Are there possibly things that laypersons—either single parents or remarried persons—might specifically offer to others?

Yes indeed. We have been implying this throughout this chapter. Now let's take a direct look. Many of us share belief in the "priesthood of believers" and the "ministry of the laity."

We are aware also that our own life experiences and hurts sometimes give rise to special gifts within ourselves that are useful to other people. For example, I once was attempting to minister to a woman who was in the intensive care unit of a hospital suffering from a severe coronary attack, and she was very frightened. She appreciated my pastoral visits but remained frightened. Then I decided on another approach. Though only family and clergy were normally allowed in the intensive care unit, I was able to bring in another person, a very perceptive and caring man in the church who also had experienced a coronary and who was leading a rather normal life. I saw the woman relax as she asked him questions and he answered out of experience. He had credibility and could offer her hope, because he had been through the same experience and was able to claim health again. On the way out of the hospital, I put my hand on his shoulder and told him, "Dave, I commission you to minister to coronaries!"

The same principle applies again and again. I have often had occasion to minister to people out of the hurt of losing my father when I was only ten years old. I seem to have a special rapport, something extra to give both to men who lost their fathers and to women who are trying to raise children without a husband.

And this principle applies to the topic at hand. Coauthor Carole is a good example. She herself was divorced, functioned as a single parent, and then remarried. Out of this experience she developed a fascination with the issues of remarriage and the resources available for remarried persons. She took what courses she could on this subject, and she read widely. She attended conferences on the subject that she saw advertised. She talked with many other remarried persons. When things were tough, she sought counsel with a good therapist, who was also remarried. The friendship with this therapist outlasted the therapy and provided her with another person with whom to consult and visit. She was coleader of her first group with coauthor Dick, then her pastor, but she has gone on to speak for many groups and be widely available to persons concerned with remarriage and stepfamilies.

So we suggest that a church might enrich itself by identifying persons who are sensitive, caring persons and who are also

—widow or widower,
—divorcee,
—single parent,
—remarried person and/or couple.

We suggest that such persons might be gathered, given training and support in peer counseling and lay ministry and then asked to undertake tasks that might include the following:

—to be special care persons, in addition to the church's care system, for any persons in the church whose experience they have shared;
—to be involved in developing special experiences and/or support groups for this population;
—to be involved in the subculture of persons who are also widowed, divorced, single parents and so on, but who are outside the church; to serve as a bridge between the church and these persons;
—to be sensitive to what the church is communicating to these persons; to listen with constructively critical ears, read with critical eyes, and let the pastor know if anything is said from the pulpit or in church publications that ignores or excludes this population of persons (this one may be difficult; many laypersons find it hard to confront their pastor, even helpfully);
—to be an advocate on behalf of this population so that intentional programming for this group may develop and all other aspects of the life of the church are kept open to them.

What Can the Clergy Do to Bring This Style of Congregational Life into Being?

The clergyperson can model inclusive thinking in regard to varying marital life-styles. He or she can keep all family life-styles in mind in pastoral care and counseling. He or she can see the possible strength and dignity in a family in any of the life-styles and can become increasingly aware of problems and issues that can be faced by all families and by each type of family structure. In the clergy's public statements he or she can exert caution to be sure that he or she avoids a stereotyped conception of "family" and that all family units feel included in statements about or in illustrations of family life.

The clergyperson can engage in intentional education and reeducation, the goal of which is to change a church's attitude, policy, and program in regard to single-parent and remarried families. The minister can, from time to time, share sermons and classes on the theology of divorce and remarriage. The minister can also offer sermons or adult-education events on the caring community and ministry to persons in stress. Bereavement, including the death of a spouse, and loss of the original family unit through divorce might be two of the topics discussed at such times.

At all church programs, the minister might include the needs of single-parent and remarried families among the topics offered to the congregation. (In the church I serve, the monthly all-church dinner would be the occasion for such a program.) Other churches would need to schedule such events on their calendars of church activities. For example, a panel discussion on family living, including persons from intact families, two-career marriages, single-parent families, remarried families, childless or empty-nest couples and single persons might occasion a new sensitivity.

The minister can, at an opportune time, request that the appropriate board develop a broad, supportive policy in regard to marital/family life-styles. Once the policy is in place, then programs can be developed to implement the policy.

Wisdom needs to be exercised as to when this will be presented. Some churches might be ready but haven't given it thought. Others may have some serious questions and need a period of board study and reflection before they are ready to make a decision. The clergy should try to identify persons who need or want special dialogue on this issue before they are ready to vote.

When proposing such policy, it is wise to put it in the larger context. Avoid a mistake I once made. I was visiting with church leaders to discuss new program thrusts that I wanted to see developed. In my enthusiasm for the needs we had been discussing, I exclaimed, "I'd like it if our church would do something about remarriage." Very quickly and quietly came the response from one leader, "I'd like it if our church would do something about marriage." I had unintentionally communicated enthusiasm for one marital life-style over another, which I should not have done. A policy that better fits the mission of the church would be a commitment to strengthening marriage and family life with all persons from the cradle to the grave. A subpoint under this broad policy would be to develop a special sensitivity and response to widowed and divorcing persons, single parents, and remarried families.

Then the minister, in cooperation with church leaders and boards, can enthusiastically apply this policy to every area of church life. Church publications can be brought into conformity with the policy. Any brochure interpreting church life to potential members might include the sentence "This church welcomes you, single, married, or remarried" or some other such phrase. Information about church members might illustrate the openness and sensitivity we have advocated earlier in this chapter.

The church library can be expanded to include resources to help single parents or remarrying persons and also to educate the rest of the church about their circumstances. Curriculum can be proposed that would include education for family living on all age levels. The circumstances of present or potential class members would be considered, as well as different family styles. Support systems within a particular family/marital life-style and among the varying life-styles might also be developed.

Strategies to include the children of widowed and divorced people and the children of remarriage can be evolved, such as:

—having children's stories or sermons on varying life-styles so that no children feel left out;

—having books in their classrooms and the church library that have similar broad understandings of family life-styles;

—training teachers on the various family styles and the sensitivities needed with the children;

—developing church school registration forms that include the name of each family member and the names they use;

—offering support groups for children whose parents have died, divorced, or remarried.[10]

The insights of this chapter and the insights that you are developing can also be applied. In addition, the following chapter provides many resources to help you carry out the suggestions of this chapter.

7

A Process Guide for a Short-Term Remarried-Couples' Group

We'd now like to share with you a guide for conducting a six-session series for remarried couples or for those about to be remarried. First, however, we share a few assumptions.

While much wider reading would be useful, we will provide a guide here that assumes the use of just two books: this volume and the authors' companion volume, *Help for Remarried Couples and Families*. This second volume is a must for the leader. It will be helpful (and couples will probably grow more) if all have copies of this study book and read the designated chapters before each session. Persons can gain from the sessions without previous reading, however. Some individuals gain much from reading, so we urge having available a wide selection from the other resources mentioned in the next chapter.

Much publicity and many individual invitations will be needed to bring this group into reality. If at all possible, remarried couples should take part in conceiving, designing, promoting, leading, and inviting participants to this series. Advertising should be upbeat, optimistic, and hopeful.

The purpose of this group is to provide helpful information and support. In many circumstances remarried couples have felt alone in their problems. Permission to talk about these issues and the awareness that other couples have similar problems will provide a great sense of relief and hope. Such a group can help couples with developmental problems but not those with deeper couple-family problems. Be ready to suggest counseling resources for such persons, in addition to their participation in this group.

Should you allow one person to come alone if the spouse does not wish to attend? Usually yes; remarried persons have memories of being single persons left out of couples' groups, and so will likely be sensitive and include the person who comes without his or her spouse. However, perhaps someone from the group could give a particularly appealing invitation to the absent spouse so that he or she will come and enter in as well.

We strongly suspect that this type of group is best led by a team, either by a male-and-female team or perhaps, a pastor-and-remarried-couple team.

But now, on to the sessions.

Session 1: Building a One-on-One Relationship in Remarriage

Goals

a. To welcome the participants, help them get acquainted with each other, and help them feel comfortable in the group

b. To form a group contract for future meetings

c. To help participants gain insight and perspective on how they began their present relationship

d. To help participants identify possible unfinished business from their mate-selection process and to discover ways to fill in these gaps in their relationship

Preparation

a. Invite carefully those who you think will benefit from this group. Use personal follow-up as well as public advertising to secure the members of the group.

b. Read chapters 4 and 5 in the study book.

c. Choose and arrange your meeting room to be as friendly, informal, and homey as possible.

The Session

Team leaders should be there early to welcome people and set them at ease as they arrive. When it seems as though everyone has arrived, sit down in a circle. Ask each couple to introduce themselves and tell how and where they met. Be sure to give opportunity for both partners to tell the story; the versions often differ!

Then take a moment to arrange the seating in a circle; each couple should sit together, but each person will also be sitting next to another person. Tell them that you are going to have them turn to the person beside them and talk to that person—not their spouses—on some topics.

You will have them turn to their spouses and discuss other topics. If there are persons without spouses, have team members join them and discuss the topics suggested.

Ask persons to turn to the person next to them who is not their spouse and discuss this topic: "Observers note that recently widowed or divorced persons often have one of these attitudes: 'Never again, I'll never marry again,' or 'I must get married again, and soon. . . . ' Which attitude did you have? What influenced it? If it changed, how and when did it change?"

Call the group back together and note that persons often have a loss of self-confidence right after being widowed or divorced. Again have the group members turn to the person not their spouse and discuss these topics: "As I compare how I felt about myself when my previous relationship ended to how I feel about myself now, here are the changes I see. . . . What in my life contributed to these changes? It was _____ years (or months) after my previous marriage ended that I entered this one. I felt ready for this in that I. . . . "

Now call the whole group together and lead them in this discussion: "People have noted that sometimes persons remarry for 'poison reasons,' that is to say for reasons of desperation. And sometimes they marry for healthy reasons. Let's make a list of the 'poison' or 'desperation' reasons for entering a remarriage and also make a list of the 'healthy' reasons." The beginning of chapter 4 in the study book provides some information to help you work with the group to draw up such lists. Do this on large newsprint so that the whole list is clearly visible to the whole group.

Now ask each person to turn to his or her spouse and discuss this: "As I look at that list, I suspect I married for these healthy reasons . . . and for these desperation reasons (if any). . . . " If the couple detect some desperation reasons in the decision to remarry, have them discuss whether these have placed extra burdens on the relationship. If so, in what ways?

Next, suggest that it might be useful to look at the ways that relationships develop. One of the leader team might want to mention and list the steps that Morton Hunt sees in a developing relationship (see study book, chapter 5). However, with the persons present, the final step was not "The Break-Up" but "Commitment." After a leader has described this process, have each person turn to his or her spouse and discuss these topics: "What were the important events in our relationship that drew us closer together? What obstacles did I experience in building a relationship with you? What was it I treasured about you and us that caused me to persist and move toward marriage in spite of those obstacles?''

For the final stage of the discussion in this session, have one of the leaders (or perhaps the remarried-couple leader team) talk about the tasks of early marriage. The authors of the study book speak of ''re-marriage shock,'' of the tasks of early marriage in general, and then of the unique tasks of *re*married couples (see chapter 5). Some may want to summarize this information or speak of their own experiences, after becoming aware of this information. Then partners should be urged to dialogue with each other in response to the following questions: ''How was our experience similar to that described? How was our experience different from that described? In the light of all we've discussed tonight, what topics do we need to discuss with each other to make our marriage even better?''

Give a chance for brief comments and feedback. Then propose a group contract with the persons present. Share the outline of sessions suggested in this guide and see if this seems to be close to the interests and needs of the group. Make necessary adjustments so that the outline fits your group. Does the group want to promise one another that they will be faithful to these sessions? Can others join the group? Next time? Any time? Would group members like to plan other activities? Would they like to plan a social get-together and include children?

If some are reading the study book, tell them to browse through chapters 1 and 3 and to read chapter 6 before the next meeting. Conclude with prayers of thanksgiving for the evening's experience and the shared journey.

Session 2: Building a Remarried-Family Structure
Goals

a. To raise remarried persons' consciousness about the complexity of the issues with which they must deal by identifying some of those issues

b. To discover the resource of self-awareness and faith for coping with these complex issues having to do with the structure, system, and process of remarriage

Preparation

a. Carefully read and absorb chapter 6 of the study book (it contains much insight as to why remarriages are so difficult).

b. Duplicate the questions at the beginning of chapter 3 in the study book and hand out to each member of the group. Collect all the necessary supplies and materials to do the activities in this session.

The Session

Begin by reading, without comment, Ephesians 4:25, twice; the second time read more slowly and emphatically, emphasizing the phrase "for we are members one of another."

Then give two tasks to the couples to work on. Create an atmosphere in which they can do these two tasks informally, talking out loud with other couples as they do them. The tasks are as follows: (a) Have the couples answer the questions that you have duplicated from chapter 3 of the study book. All can answer questions 1-10. Some may have problems with questions 11-14. Since you will have read chapter 3 in the study book, you will be able to give the couples some guidance on possible answers to those questions. (b) Have them draw their family network on a fairly large piece of blank paper. See, for example, "Henry and Carole's Family Network" at the end of chapter 6 in the study book. Have them use the same symbols. We are going to do some other things with this network chart later, so have them make it rather large.

When all have finished with those two tasks, start by simply asking people to respond to each of the questions on the questionnaire. On the questions for which a simple answer is indicated, have couples raise hands on the answer that is accurate for them. Quite likely, for some questions the couples will have the same answers and for some they will have different answers. The discovery from this exercise might simply be the number of variations there are in remarried families. Invite comments and insights when you have finished.

Then, ask each couple to study their family-network chart. Ask them what they notice, what they conclude as they look at the chart. One discovery might be the number of people with whom they must inter-act—the number of people whose destiny is somehow tied to their own. There may be many other discoveries. Then have couples do three more things with their charts:

—Have them encircle (with one continuous line) all the persons on the chart whom each spouse and each spouse's children include in their definition of family. The configurations may vary for each spouse and each child. Somehow label these groups so that everyone can see who is in each person's "family."

—Next, draw a circle or partial circle around the name of each person that husband or wife includes in his or her family. If the person is there all the time, draw a full circle; if there one-tenth of the time, draw one-tenth of a circle, and so on.

—Next give each couple red, green, and blue crayons. Tell them to mark each name with colors. If the person is enthusiastic about the remarriage and the stepfamily, mark the name with red; if the person is opposed or resisting, mark the name with green; if the person is indifferent or has an attitude that is unknown, mark the name with blue. (Some persons may be a combination of two or three colors.

Discuss the discoveries that come from doing these tasks: there may be no single definition of who is in the family and who is not; probably a number of families are experiencing opposition of some important people to the family structure; and remarried families have personnel who are present from time to time and this calls for special strategies for including the persons who may be there only briefly. (See chapter 5 in the study book for discussion and suggestions on these issues).

Next, have group members draw a house around the persons that are present most of the time (even if it is an oddly shaped house). Point out that families sometimes have issues over housing in remarriage. Ask them to discuss how they arranged housing. Did they move into one partner's home? If so, did the newcomers feel a part of it? How was this achieved? Did they purchase (or rent) different housing from what either had? If so, what entered into that decision? Did housing contribute to building the new family unit? If so, how? What issues of space did they face and resolve?

Then go on to point out other issues in remarriage family structure. Discuss with your group the concept of remarriage and stepfamilies as "unfinished institutions" (see chapter 6, in the study book). Ask persons in what ways they have experienced uncertainty in remarriage because it is an "unfinished institution."

Point out the fact that competing family loyalties play a part in remarried families. Note the six family expectations that Phoebe and Rick's family brought to their remarriage (see "Issue 2" in chapter 6 of the study book). Ask if the couples have experienced these. If so, what issues were involved? How did they resolve these issues?

Conclude by asking, "If remarriage and stepfamilies are very complex, what resources do you need for succeeding in the delicate and difficult tasks that are involved?" We would contend that one of the resources is simply making visible what is actually going on. Be sure to suggest faith resources including prayer (see the story at the end of chapter 6 in the study book) and the insight of Ephesians 4:25 (also discussed at the end of chapter 6 in the study book).

You might want to create a spontaneous litany. Have different persons mention the issues remarried families face. After each issue is mentioned, have all respond, "And yet, we are members one of another." Repeat this until no more issues are mentioned.

Assign the reading of chapter 7 in the study book (for those using this book) for the next session.

Session 3: Remarriage and Children

Goals

a. To give permission to talk about issues involving children and to create a nonthreatening atmosphere in which this can be done (probably a hot issue for at least some participants)

b. To encourage remarried couples to be resource persons to other remarried couples on this and other issues

The method suggested for this session is rather "gutsy." For some it might be wise and/or easier and/or more appropriate to do a straightforward discussion of the eight issues mentioned in chapter 7 of the study book, using the questions at the end of the chapter and adding a few more. However, the following design is aimed at getting persons to express how and where they are really hurting in the area of child-rearing and to put persons who need the most help in this area in touch with those who are most resourceful. We urge you to give it a try.

Preparation

a. Reading chapter 7 in the study book and everything else you can on successful stepparenting. (See resources listed in the next chapter.)

b. If possible, recruit a remarried couple or two who have succeeded in building a strong family life and relating to each other's children to join the evening as resource person/participants.

c. Prepare the materials and collect the supplies indicated in the process.

The Session

As people arrive, ask them to examine the charts you have prepared and have placed on the walls around the room. Tell them to put a sentence, a phrase, a word about how they handle this situation in the family in the center, blank section of each chart. Tell them to be sure to put a check across each of the two bottom lines, one indicating the importance they give this issue, the other indicating their success in dealing with it.

Here is what you have prepared for them: Large newsprint sheets with one issue (as described in the next paragraph) at the top of each sheet. The center section is blank. Across the bottom, there are two scales:

Importance:
_____
not important at all   so-so   very important

Success:
_____
feel like failure   struggling   ???   small signs of success   great!

Make sure people understand they can put their check mark anywhere along the line, including a place where someone else has put a check mark.

The statements to have at the top of the sheets are these:

1. The couple need to give primacy to their own relationship so that they will have strength to deal with their children.
2. Names, what adults call the children and what children call the adults, are important concerns in stepfamilies.
3. Children often resist remarriages and show this by sullenness, disobedience, and name-calling.
4. Discipline is frequently a hotly debated topic in stepfamilies. Who decides what discipline is to be used and when? Who administers discipline?
5. Stepbrothers/sisters often have intense rivalries that are difficult to cope with.
6. It is difficult to know what to do when a child of divorced-remarried parents gets into difficulty.
7. Sexual matters (privacy, modesty, incest—whether in fantasy or in various types of acting out) are important issues in the stepfamily.

And so, for the first part of this activity, each individual examines each statement, puts in comments, and checks how important the issue is and how successfully she or he has dealt with it. Tell them that we will come back to these sheets shortly.

Then propose three rounds of "fishbowl" discussion. In each, certain people are invited to join in a conversation in the center of a circle. Other persons sit in an outer circle and listen/observe. (Allow 10 minutes or so for each round.)

First, invite all stepmothers into the fishbowl. Ask them to comment on the experience of being a stepmother. What are the joys? What are the problems? What have been unexpected issues? Does the fairy-tale or television image of "wicked stepmother" haunt them? How do they feel about being stepmothers?

Second, invite all stepfathers into the fishbowl. What is it like being a stepfather? Where do they feel included and where left out? Are there tough financial issues involved in being a stepfather? What unexpected joys and/or what unexpected problems have they experienced as stepfathers?

Third, invite all "hybrid parents" (those who have both biological children and stepchildren), both male and female parents, into the fishbowl. Ask them to compare being a biological parent to being a stepparent. Do they have problems with differences in feelings? Treatment? What joys, surprises, or unexpected issues did they experience in combining these roles?

You may have left out a few who are biological parents only. You might want to invite them into the "fishbowl" and ask what it feels like to share parenting with someone who is not a biological parent of their children.

When all have finished, invite comment and dialogue about what they have discovered about others' tasks in child rearing.

Next, turn your attention to the charts. Select those that seem to have high interest. If there are checks indicating that someone feels very unsuccessful and someone feels very successful, discover who the two persons (or couples) are and invite them to dialogue about that issue. Help both parties clearly understand and communicate with each other. When the two parties have finished, invite comment, shared experiences, and further suggestions from others.

We suspect that a lively discussion will occur and that you will run out of time. If so, the discussion should be continued at the next meeting, for you are dealing with what remarried people identify as their number one issue. We would suggest starting with easier issues and moving on to harder ones (discipline, a child in trouble, and sexual matters are probably the hardest). Perhaps participants will know of other remarried couples who have faced crises in these areas and coped well and will want to invite them to share with the group.

Close with a devotional sharing that there are faith resources to help deal with such issues, particularly the Ephesians image of the church, which described previously unrelated persons as becoming family in Christ (Ephesians 2:19), and the Galatians image of Christians as persons adopted into the family of God (Galatians 4:5b-7). (See a discussion of these faith resources in the study book in chapter 7).

Those who are reading the study book should read chapter 8 for the next meeting. All should be given copies of the four charts in that chapter and urged to fill in what they can before the next meeting. Tell them to come to the meeting even if they can't complete all the information required to fill in the charts.

Session 4: Money and Remarriage

Goals

a. To open up communication between partners about money

b. To help couples identify and isolate the money issues that may be troubling them

c. To help couples develop strategies and take the first steps to resolve their money issues

Preparation

a. Have extra copies of the various financial forms available for those who do not have them.

b. Have available copies of the attitude survey in chapter 8.

c. Have the following sayings printed in large letters on newsprint and post them around the meeting room:

"The love of money is the root of all evil."—1 Timothy 6:10

"The lack of money is the root of all evil."—George Bernard Shaw

"It's a kind of spiritual snobbery that makes people think they can be happy without money."—Albert Camus

"Three items that every newlywed couple should have are a commonsense book on sex, a practical cookbook, and a good book on personal finance."[1]

d. Have a circle of chairs facing the chalkboard or newsprint. These chairs should be movable so that each couple can, in turn, turn and speak quietly and privately to each other or face in and be part of the larger group.

The Session

Begin by briefly telling the story of how the issue of money surfaced in Carole and Henry's experience as recorded at the beginning of chapter 8 in the study book.

Then ask couples to turn to each other and for ten minutes discuss the financial situations and attitudes they brought to their marriage. To guide them, hand each couple a small sheet of paper with these questions on it: "What financial assets and liabilities did each of us bring to our marriage? Did we have a hard time telling each other about our finances or making financial plans together? Did we have a prenuptial financial agreement? If so, are there things we would change if we could rewrite it with the wisdom we now have? What would we have said in it? Do we have any unsolved financial issues?"

Give the group a few moments to comment on insights or discoveries from their one-on-one discussions.

Next invite the couples to explore their present day-to-day financial management. Make sure each couple has a copy of the chart of sources of income from the study book ("Form I Family Income"). If they have already completed it, have them go over it to be sure both understand all the items and agree on the information recorded. If they have not filled it in previously, have them do this quickly. For any items of which they are not sure, have them put an estimate and then a question mark beside the number so that they can verify it later. (This procedure would apply in the next steps also.)

Next, give them the chart "Form II Fixed Expenses—Including Savings." Have them either complete this or discuss it, and arrive at the amount they have for everyday expenses ("Form III Day-to-Day Expenses").

Then give them the chart for budgeting everyday expenses ("Form IV Budgeting Day-to-Day Expenses"). Again encourage them to fill it out or examine and discuss what they have already filled out.

When they have completed these steps, hand each couple a copy of the following questions for a few minutes of discussion: "As I look at these charts, what makes me happy? What makes me worried or upset? What would I like to change about our financial situation? What would I like to add, reduce, or omit? What specific changes would I like to make in the way we manage our money and what we do with it?''

At this point you might want to draw the whole group together. You might suggest that perhaps some couples are facing issues that other couples have resolved. Ask if any couple has an issue on which they would like some input. If there is no response, you might ask couples if they have faced any financial issues that they have resolved.

This section deals with important but difficult issues. If the group is lively and is talking with a sense of involvement and earnestness, let it flow and do not push on to complete the other items suggested for this session. The group may be feeling so much relief in finding some handles on these issues that it would be a shame to short circuit the process.

Perhaps at an appropriate point you can lead the discussion in this direction: "When we talk about money, it seems that we talk about more than money as well. What other issues are involved?" Ask the group, "What are some of the more-than-money issues that come up in discussions on money? What are some of the more-than-money issues that emerge in remarried families when money is discussed?" Use the discussion of these issues in chapter 8 in the study book to help persons be aware that emotional, conflictual, cultural issues enter into attitudes and conversations about money.

You might then invite couples to turn to each other and share their financial histories briefly. You might hand the partners these questions and ask each to share with the other their responses to them: "When I was a child, the attitude toward money in my family was. . . . Two or three people that most strongly influenced my attitude toward money were. . . . Two or three events that most strongly influenced my attitude toward money were. . . . '' (There is a longer list of topics on financial history in chapter 8 of the study book.)

Perhaps you will also want to provide the time for partners to do the value exercise on attitudes toward money in chapter 8. Encourage them to discuss the question, "Where are we similar and where are we different in regard to our attitudes toward money?"

Then, as you draw near the conclusion of your session, you might want to ask the partners of each couple to discuss with each other, "What specific steps can we take to improve our financial life together? How do we put these steps in action? When will we evaluate how we are doing?" Some couples might want to share their decisions with other couples as part of expressing their commitment to make these decisions work. (They might not want to do this because financial decisions feel very private to some people. No one should be forced.)

You might want to close the session with a brief devotional thought on life as stewardship-managership. We live life, not only for ourselves, but for each other, our children, and God. The core of such a devotional thought is found in the last two paragraphs of chapter 8 in the study book.

This session on money issues in remarriage could easily be expanded into three or four sessions on money management.

Session A: At a more leisurely pace explore each person's financial history, attitudes toward money, and what each partner of a couple brought to the marriage. Have partners fill out the financial management sheets for their present marriage before this session.

Session B: Invite a financial counselor from a bank or some other financial agency to discuss family money management; go through the charts with the couples and answer any questions.

Session C: Have an attorney come in and discuss wills, insurance, and provision for one's family after one has died.

Session D: Have a financial-planning consultant speak to the group about savings and investment.

Identify your group's financial questions and needs and attempt to build sessions responsive specifically to them.

Session 5: Anger and Conflict in Remarriage
Goals

    a. To examine the participants' experience of anger and conflict in a nonthreatening situation removed from an actual conflict

    b. To help participants develop awareness of different styles of conflict that may be occurring in their relationship

    c. To help participants unlearn some bad habits in conflict and learn some good ones

Preparation

    a. Become thoroughly acquainted with chapter 9 in the study book and possibly other material on conflict management.

    b. Prepare suggested charts.

    c. Secure a couple to do the "controlled role play" and practice it.

The Session

When people arrive, have two signs posted, one on one wall and one on the opposite wall. One sign will read, "Conflict is painful, hurtful, destructive." The other sign will read, "Conflict is helpful, relationship-building, useful." On the floor midway between the two put a sign that says, "Conflict is neutral." Ask people to arrange themselves along this line. The more closely they identify with the statement on a sign, the closer they place themselves to it. They should not stand directly in the center; they need to decide which side of center they choose. Then invite persons to talk with persons closest to them about why they chose that particular position. It is likely that persons will be more concentrated on the negative side.

Then lead a brief discussion about where our attitudes toward conflict originate. You might raise these questions: "What did you learn about conflict in your childhood home from what your parents explicitly taught you? from your parents' example? from your own experience? What did you experience/learn about conflict in your former marriage?" If group members choose to talk about it, they will probably report some destructive, disruptive experiences. If they choose not to talk about it, assume that some persons have had such experiences and go on to the next steps.

Point out that if there is to be successful conflict in marriage, two things must happen. First, people need to recognize that different people have different styles of participating in conflict. Each couple needs to know how both partners prefer to act out or express conflict. Engage the group in making a list of how two people can differ in the way they participate in conflict. (See chapter 9 of study book for a list of some of these differences. A group can certainly expand that list.) Point out that when partners are aware of their different styles of conflicting, they can discuss in advance of a conflict what method they will use when differences between them occur. And when conflict is occurring, they may feel freer to ask, "What's going on here?" (Do not ask persons for self-disclosure on these delicate matters.) Invite couples to take a few minutes to discuss with each other the statement "We tend to differ in our conflict styles in these ways."

Second, persons need to get rid of bad habits in conflict situations and develop some better habits. Ask the group's help to make a list of bad habits people develop in conflict. Ask each individual to make a list; then compile the list on newsprint, large enough for all to see. Write only on the left side of the paper. After you have made the list of bad habits, write opposite each one what the good habit in conflict management would be. (See discussion in chapter 9). Do this as a group.

Then do the "controlled," prerehearsed role play with a couple you have selected. Suggest to the group that this couple is going to explore the steps on conflict management in remarriage that the authors of the study book have distilled from their thinking and experience. Have a narrator announce or describe each step. Then have the couple do it.

1. Build individual self-esteem. (Each partner tells the other two or three things she or he really values in the partner.)

2. Affirm and strengthen your relationship with each other. (Each partner tells the other what he or she values in the relationship and then affirms the commitment to make it work even when conflict comes.)

3. Ask yourselves, "Is this conflict a result of my relationship with my present spouse or is it a carry over from a previous relationship? Is it due to displaced anger?" (Have one partner carry on a soliloquy on this and conclude that this conflict is indeed one that belongs to this relationship.)

4. Admit, accept, and take responsibility for your own anger. (Have the same partner do a soliloquy about this also. Have the person include some reflection on how hard it is to say, "I'm angry," and what in our culture and background makes it so hard.)

5. Confront the person with whom you are angry. (The narrator here explains the issue in this conflict if it has not come up yet. The couple may select their own issue, or they may want to use an imaginary one. Here's one if they don't have their own: A couple have agreed that they want to redo their backyard. One wants to do it so that it is as little work as possible and has lots of play areas for various sports—maybe even a swimming pool. The other wants it to be a beautiful area with Japanese garden, rose garden, herb garden, vegetable garden, and so on. Have the confronter do the confronting in two different styles as narrator introduces them. First, do it with "you" messages—put downs, name calling, and so forth. Then, do it with "I" messages—what the person is feeling, wanting, and needing at this time.)

6. Agree on a style for "fair fighting." (Assume that the couple accepts the list the group has made and do not tarry here.)

7. Explore the issues. (Let both partners argue persuasively for what they want in this back yard. Let them do so as hard as they can but cleanly, without attacks. Perhaps they both can have sketches of how the backyard would look in their plan, large enough for the group to see. Have them test what is really important to each one and what they can let go.)

8. Ask yourselves what it would take to resolve this situation. (Per-

haps each partner could state one or two things that he or she must
have in this backyard. Perhaps they can agree to a plan that includes
some space for each and leaves some space open for future plans.)

9. Agree what solution you will try and for what period of time.
(Have the couple appear to draw a sketch, actually prepared in advance,
that includes some ideas from both; have them agree to first steps on
a dated timetable. Each partner will check it out with the other and
then both will agree.

10. Kiss and make up. Celebrate. (Have the couple do so, congrat-
ulating each other on their best strategies and points and getting very
cozy.)

Briefly mention that the authors have an eleventh point. They suggest
that if a couple seem to be failing in conflict management, they should
seek competent professional marriage counseling, which can provide a
structured, sheltered way to work out conflict.

Invite comment and observations from the group. Then ask the
members to arrange themselves along the spectrum with which you
began the session. After they have chosen their spaces, ask if any have
moved in the course of the session. Tell them that your goal was to get
them to take at least a step toward the appreciation of conflict as a
marriage-building activity. Reach out, hold hands, and close with prayers
of reconciliation and healing. For those using the study book, assign
chapter 2 for the next session.

Session 6: Remarriage and Religion

Goals

a. To help participants deal with diversity of religious preference

b. To help participants deal with the guilt or anger they may feel
toward church or God out of their experience of divorce/widowhood/
remarriage

c. To help participants explore the possibility of spiritual growth
within their remarriage

Preparation

a. Acquaint yourself with chapter 2 of the study book and chapter 1
of this book.

b. Recruit persons from within the group or out of it who might have
something explicit to share about their spiritual pilgrimage in divorce/
widowhood/remarriage.

The Session

Begin by presenting the following dilemma and brainstorming possible responses.

Jane and Bob have decided to marry; it is the second marriage for both. For various reasons both have been inactive in their churches for some time but feel a desire to return. Jane and Bob each have two children, a boy and a girl. These children have grown up mostly outside the church but are open to their parents' desire to make religion more of a force in their family life. Jane has roots and feels comfortable in the _____ church and Bob has roots and feels equally comfortable in the _____ church. (Select two religious groups of marked difference that are known in your part of the country.) List all of the decisions this couple could make about religion.

Make sure the group sticks with this task long enough to come up with as complete a list as possible. Then ask the group to consider the various diversities in religion that a remarrying couple could experience (for example: believer-nonbeliever, practicer-nonpracticer, and so on).

Invite comment in response to the following questions: "Are there couples here who represent religious diversity in one or more of these ways? If so, how are you dealing with it? Does this style feel good to you? Can you imagine other ways to deal with this diversity that might be as good or better for you?"

When it feels appropriate, move on to another topic. Suggest they examine their relationship with their church as they went through divorce (or being widowed) and beginning a new marriage. What support or lack of it did they feel from church when their previous marriage ended, for whatever reason? What help or resources (or lack of them) did they experience as single persons and possibly as single parents?

Their experiences may be very mixed or mostly negative. Perhaps the leader can help people see the balance in these, or perhaps the leader will need to express sorrow at what they have experienced, ask forgiveness on behalf of the church and point out that this particular group is an effort on the part of the church to be more responsive and supportive.

Go on and explore with them what they experienced in their relationship with God as they went through the breakup of an old relationship and subsequently the building of a new one. Some people find this a time when they feel cut off from God and spiritual growth. Others find such times, with all their uncertainty and vulnerability, to be profoundly meaningful religious experiences. Elicit response and sharing here. Perhaps you will have persons prepared to speak in some detail about their own experience of the religious dimension of their divorce/widowhood and their remarriage.

It might be helpful to explore Jesus' teachings about divorce as discussed thoroughly in chapter 1 of this book and summarized in chapter 2 of the study book.

Then lead them on to the topic of possible spiritual growth within this relationship. Ask them to cooperate in trying one experience of building spiritual community and growth between them.

Have couples sit together, each with pencil and paper. Ask each person to write for five to ten minutes on any one of the following topics: (1) What my religion means to me; (2) A person that profoundly influenced me was _____; how did that person influence me? (3) An event in my life that deeply influenced how I believe was _____ (4) What do I really stand for and what significance does this hold for me? Then invite the partners to read what they have written, to each other only. Have the listener respond only with questions for more information or clarification, not with judgments. After they have done this, ask them to comment on the meaning of the experience.

It is hoped that this sharing of deep places in their lives might contribute to their spiritual life together. Ask them to think of other ways that a couple can grow religiously and spiritually together (chapter 2 in the study book offers some suggestions for ways to share.)

Conclude by thanking the group members for sharing this pilgrimage. Perhaps decisions need to be made. Would this group like to continue? Would they like to get together for a party or some other event? Would they like to form an ongoing support group? Would some like to help offer such an experience to other remarried couples? Would some like to help plan other couple/family enrichment events for the whole church?

Ask couples to join hands and close with a prayer of thanksgiving, celebration, and petition that God's intention of one-flesh marriages might be known in all of their relationships.

8

Resources for the Church's Ministry with Remarried People

We trust that by now your mind is humming with possibilities for creative and healing ministries with all types of marriages, life-styles, and families within your congregation.

One task remains for us: to put you in touch with the resources of which we are aware and which may aid you in whatever ministries and program thrusts you choose to develop. We shall offer resource suggestions in connection with the particular concerns and programs we have suggested.

We will describe resources in one of two ways—either a simple listing or a listing plus a few sentences of explanation. The latter form simply means that we have used this resource extensively in our work and so can tell a bit about its usefulness to us. We are not implying disapproval by a simple listing. We are just including resources that we have seen briefly or that have been recommended to us by people we trust. We hope that this list (though brief and suggestive and certainly not including all worthy materials) will be well-rounded enough to give you a start when you want to increase sensitivity and establish program.

Resources to Aid in the Healthy Recovery from the Grief of Death/Divorce and the Loss of a First Marriage

Support for Widows/Widowers

Burgess-Kohn, Jane, and Kohn, Willard K., *The Widower*. Boston: Beacon Press, 1979.

Caine, Lynn, *Widow*. New York: Bantam Books, Inc., 1974.

Detrich, Richard L., and Steele, Nicola J., *How to Recover from Grief*. Valley Forge: Judson Press, 1983.

Johnson, Nancy K., *Alone and Beginning Again*. Valley Forge: Judson Press, 1982.

Kreis, Bernadine, and Pattie, Alice. *Up from Grief: Patterns of Recovery*. New York: The Seabury Press, 1969.

Lewis, C. S., *A Grief Observed*. New York: Bantam Books Inc., 1976.

Oates, Wayne E., *Pastoral Care and Counseling in Grief and Separation*. Philadelphia: Fortress Press, 1976.

Silverman, Phyllis, *et al., Helping Each Other in Widowhood*. New York: Health Sciences Publishing Corp., 1974.

Wylie, Betty Jane, *Beginnings: A Book for Widows*. Toronto: McClelland and Stewart Ltd., 1978.

Support for Divorced People

Dalke, David, *The Healing Divorce: A Practical and Theological Approach*. Available from Learnings Unlimited, 516 4th Avenue., Longmont, CO 80501. Dalke, an ordained United Methodist minister, has created a model of divorce recovery using the story of liberation of the children of Israel found in the biblical book of Exodus. He provides input on tapes and then suggests a group process in an accompanying workbook entitled *The Healing Divorce Guidebook*. He also includes a tape of background information and insight for clergy. Dalke's material was the most intentional dialogue between biblical faith and the circumstance of the divorced persons that we located.

Fisher, Bruce, *Rebuilding: When Your Relationship Ends*. San Luis Obispo, Calif.: Impact Publishers, Inc., 1981. This is Fisher's readable description of the fifteen building blocks of divorce recovery that he located in doctoral research. The book is a valuable discussion tool. Fisher conducts training seminars for persons who want more insight in using his concepts and process. For information about these, write Family Relations Learning Center, 450 Ord Drive, Boulder, CO 80303.

Krantzler, Mel, *Creative Divorce*. New York: The New American Library, Inc., Signet Books, 1975; and *Learning to Love Again: Beyond Creative Divorce*. New York: Harper & Row, Publishers, Inc., Thomas Y. Crowell, 1977. Krantzler also offers workshops to train persons in groups using his insights and methods. For more information contact Creative Divorce/Learning to Love Again National Counseling Center, 610 D Street, San Rafael, CA 94901.

Support for Single-Parent Families

For Adults

Klein, Carole, *The Single Parent Experience*. New York: Avon Books, 1973.

Murdock Carol, *Single Parents Are People, Too*. New York: Butterick Publishing, 1980.

Spilke, Francine S., *What About the Children—A Divorced Parent's Handbook*. New York: Crown Publishers, Inc., 1979.

Weiss, Robert G., *Going It Alone—The Family Life and Social Situation of the Single Parent*. New York: Basic Books, Inc., Publishers, 1979.

For Teenagers

Blume, Judy, *It's Not the End of the World*. Bradbury Press, 1972.

Gardner, Richard A., *The Boys and Girls Book About One-Parent Families*. New York: G. P. Putnam's Sons, 1978.

Spilke, Francine S., *What About Me? Understanding Your Parent's Divorce*. New York: Crown Publishers, Inc., 1979.

For Young Children

Gardner, Richard A., *The Boys and Girls Book About Divorce*, New York: Jason Aronson, Inc., 1971.

Hazen, Barbara Shook, *Two Homes to Live In: A Child's Eye View of Divorce*. Human Sciences Press, Inc., 1978.

Spilke, Francine S., *The Family That Changed: A Child's Book About Divorce*. New York: Crown Publishers, Inc., 1979.

The Church's Ministry with Singles, Including Single Parents

Baptist Leader, vol. 45, no. 1 (April 1983). Most of this issue is devoted to the church's ministry with single adults. The following suggestions come from its bibliography.

Brown, Raymond K. *Reach Out to Singles: A Challenge to Ministry*. Philadelphia: The Westminster Press, 1979.

Carter, Velma T., and Leavenworth, J. Lynn, *Putting the Pieces Together: Help for Single Parents*. Valley Forge: Judson Press, 1977.

Christoff, Nicholas, *Saturday Night, Sunday Morning: Singles and the Church*. New York: Harper and Row, Publishers, Inc., 1980.

Claussen, Russell, ed., *The Church's Growing Edge: Single Adults*. New York: The Pilgrim Press, United Church Press, 1980.

Etzler, Carole, *Single*. Joint Educational Development, 1980. A three minute motion picture on the struggle of singles for acceptance in the church. Available from American Baptist Films, Valley Forge, PA 19481, or Box 23204, Oakland, CA 94623.

Landgraf, John R., *Creative Singlehood and Pastoral Care*. Philadelphia: Fortress Press, 1982.

Lyon, William, *A Pew for One, Please: The Church and the Single Person*. New York: The Seabury Press, Inc., 1977.

We would urge persons to contact First Baptist Church, 3033 MacVicar, Topeka, Kansas, for information about the resources and training conferences they offer to aid churches in the ministry with single persons.

Aid in Planning Remarriage Weddings

Frankly, this is a touchy topic. We didn't find much help and thus consider the chapter in this book (chapter 3)—although we struggled with it—the most complete resource for Christian remarriage weddings.

Brill, Mordecai L.; Halpin, Marlene; and Genne, William H., *Write Your Own Wedding*. Chicago: Follett Publishing Co., 1979. We recommend this guide to weddings in general.

Emerson, James G., *Divorce, the Church, and Remarriage*. Philadelphia: The Westminster Press, 1961. Contains theological reflections with implications for the creation of a remarriage service.

Fields, Susan H., *Getting Married Again*. New York: Dodd, Mead & Co., 1975. Remarriage etiquette from a secular point of view.

Hickman, Hoyt, *Ritual in a New Day: An Invitation.* Nashville: Abingdon Press, 1976. Although this book does not speak directly about remarriage ceremonies, it offers a section on rituals for the divorced and a section on endings and beginnings.

Kysar, Myrna and Robert, *The Asundered: Biblical Teachings on Divorce and Remarriage*. Atlanta: John Knox Press, 1978. Contains theological reflections with implications for creating a remarriage service.

Stewart, Marjabelle Y., *The New Etiquette Guide to Getting Married Again*. New York: Avon Books, 1981. Also presented from a secular point of view.

Aid for the Remarried Couple

Beginning with a Broad Marriage/Family Policy in the Church

We repeat that we believe in the wisdom of having a broad vision, policy, program in the church; we believe in a vision that encompasses enriching marriages and families of all types across the lifespan. Two resources that might be useful to help you do that are:

Leonard, Joe, Jr., *Planning Family Ministry*, Valley Forge: Judson Press, 1982. Leonard explores the tasks of family ministry, the content areas and skill areas of family living, biblical foundations, changing families, and steps to a comprehensive family ministry.

Otto, Herbert A., ed., *Marriage and Family Enrichment: New Perspectives and Programs*. Nashville: Abingdon Press, 1976. A virtual encyclopedia of possibilities. This book provides an overview of the marriage-and-family-enrichment movement, a description of many specific programs, and guidance on how to obtain further information about programs that interest the reader.

Marriage in General

Because remarrying couples have much in common with couples marrying for the first time, literature on marriage relationship in general can provide resources for remarriage relationships. We suggest these as among the most helpful that we read:

Campbell, Susan M., *The Couple's Journey: Intimacy as a Path to Wholeness*. San Luis Obispo, Calif.: Impact Publishers, Inc., 1980. This is a look at the journey process through which couples pass, if they keep growing in regard to one another.

Mace, David and Vera, *How To Have A Happy Marriage*. Nashville, Abingdon Press, 1977. A step-by-step workbook that takes a couple through the topics of relationship, communication, conflict, and growth plans for their marriage. We also suggest their book *We Can Have Better Marriages If We Really Want Them*. Nashville: Abingdon Press, 1974.

Molton, Warren L., *Friends, Partners, and Lovers: A Good Word About Marriage*. Valley Forge: Judson Press, 1979. An examination of six models of marriage and then a specific examination of marriage as a friendship, as a partnership, and as a growing love relationship.

The Remarriage Relationship in Particular

Because the remarried couple must deal with each other's families from previous marriages, there is much more written on the stepfamily than on remarriage as such. Emily and John Visher are persons who clearly state that the remarried relationship must be given priority if the stepfamily is to survive. Clifford Sager and associates examine the couple's task of setting appropriate priorities in their relationship. These works, however, are listed under the broader categories more typical of their contents.

We attempted to create the companion volume to this one specifically for persons who have remarried or are considering remarriage. In it we concentrated on the couple and their relationship. We also gave attention to the family issues that the couple will face, attempting to keep the focus throughout on how the couple could deal with each other on all these matters.

Olson, Richard P., and Della Pia-Terry, Carole, *Help for Remarried Couples and Families*. Valley Forge: Judson Press, 1984.

Aid for Stepfamilies

Easily Read Nontechnical Books for Stepfamily Members

There is much more material available when one turns from remarriage to the stepfamily. Some that we read and found useful are the following:

Burt, Mala S. and Roger B., *What's Special About Our Stepfamily: A Participation Book for Children*. New York: Doubleday & Co., Inc., 1983.

Capaldi, Fredrick, and McRae, Barbara, *Stepfamilies: A Cooperative Responsibility*. New York: Franklin Watts, Inc., New Viewpoints, 1979.

Maddox, Brenda, *The Half-Parent*. New York: The New American Library, Inc., Signet Books, 1975.

Reed, Bobby, *Stepfamilies—Living in Christian Harmony*. St. Louis: Concordia Publishing House, 1980.

Roosevelt, Ruth, and Lofas, Jeannette, *Living in Step*. New York: McGraw-Hill, Inc., 1976.

Visher, Emily B. and John S., *How to Win as a Stepfamily*. New York: Dembner Books, 1982.

Readings for the Knowledgeable Professional Working with Stepfamilies

On Counseling, Treatment, and Care of Stepfamilies and Remarriages

Sager, Clifford J. *et al.*, *Treating the Remarried Family*. New York: Brunner/Mazel, Inc., 1983. This excellent volume provides a theory of remarried families and couples (including a discussion of the differences between nuclear and remarried families), a description of treatment of remarried families, and an exploration of many of the special issues remarried families face.

Visher, Emily B., and John S., *Stepfamilies: A Guide to Working with Stepparents and Stepchildren*. New York: Brunner/Mazel, Inc., 1979. This excellent volume examines the cultural and structural characteristics of stepfamilies and then examines the special circumstances of women, men, couples, children, and stepfamilies. In each case a chapter is devoted to what that population experiences in stepfamilies, and another chapter is devoted to how to work with that population.

Wynn, J. C. *Family Therapy in Pastoral Ministry*. San Francisco: Harper & Row, Publishers, Inc., 1982. Not a book on remarried families but on family theory, this volume prepares the church professional for dealing with the complexity of systems in intact and remarried families.

Sociological Perspective on Remarried Families

Bernard, Jessie, *Remarriage: A Study of Marriage*. New York: Russell & Russell, Publishers, 1956, 1971. The pioneering work on the subject.

Duberman, Lucile, *The Reconstituted Family: A Study of Remarried Couples and Their Children*. Chicago: Nelson-Hall Publishers, 1975. Primary research by questionnaire and interview of eighty-eight remarried families in Cleveland, Ohio.

The Church's Ministry with Remarried Families

Again, we drew a blank. Most material we read on the subject of the church's ministry with remarried persons ended with the moral, theological, and ethical dilemmas of participating in the wedding, and so we developed our set of resources to fill this vacuum. We were told by one person who founded a community-based support group for remarried couples that he found the following resource exceedingly useful:

Visher, Emily B. and Visher, John S., *A Stepfamily Workshop Manual*. Stepfamily Association of California, Inc., 1980.

We invite persons who develop programs, write on this subject, or discover helpful literature to contact us through our publisher. In any future reprints of this book, we would like to provide a more complete bibliography, particularly on this topic.

Audio-Visual Resources that Might Be Used in
Programs with Remarried Couples or Families

Simon, Neil, *Chapter Two*. New York: Random House, Inc., 1979. In
this semiautobiographical play, Neil Simon directs his well-known
wit and insight to the issues of bereavement and remarriage. There
are several sections that might be read aloud and followed by discussion.

Stepparenting. 16mm film, color. Polymorph Films, 331 Newberry
Street, Boston.

Groups and Organizations that Might Provide Resources or
Be Points of Referral for the Church Professional

Remarrieds, Inc., P.O. Box 742, Santa Ana, CA 92702. This organization has a number of chapters that provide social activities, educational speakers, discussions, and community activities for remarried
persons.

The Stepfamily Association of America Inc., 900 Welch Road, Suite
400, Palo Alto, CA 94304. This organization has local chapters that
provide a support network and advocacy groups for stepfamilies. The
national and state divisions of this group have been instrumental in
starting a wide variety of services, including self-help groups, lec-
tures, meetings, and educational workshops.

Ministry of Laypersons Who Are Widowed/Divorced and Remarried, to Others in the Same Circumstances

To our knowledge, there is no material written specifically to prepare
widowed, divorced, and remarried persons to offer lay ministry to peers
in similar circumstance. However, there is material on the subject of
lay ministry that would be readily applicable to the remarried person
who has become knowledgeable about the process and wants to reach
out to others. Some of those resources include the following:

Grantham, Rudolph, E., *Lay Shepherding*. Valley Forge: Judson Press,
1980. A guide for visiting the sick, the aged, the troubled, and the
bereaved. Grantham includes the broken relationship among the bereavement situations that he discusses.

Southard, Samuel. *Training Church Members for Pastoral Care*. Valley
Forge: Judson Press, 1982.

Welter, Paul, *How to Help a Friend*, Wheaton, Ill.: Tyndale House
Publishers, 1978. Welter helps people discover how to be aware,

express warmth, identify needs, build on strengths, and respond to crises.

The Most Valuable Resource

In listing all these printed or media resources, we do not mean to overlook the most valuable resource available; we trust that you will not miss that resource either. Of course, we are referring to people— people who are widowed, people who are divorced, people who are in remarried families. Talk to them. Ask them what they are experiencing, what they need from the church, where the church is hurting them, and where the church is helping them. Talking with people, reading books, and reflecting on our feelings and experiences have led us to the insights we have shared with you. We trust that the same process will lead you on to yet more insights and creative ministry with remarried persons.

We have shared the best that we have discovered with you. And now we pray that peace, grace, and power are with you as you develop an increasingly effective churchwide ministry with all families, including remarried families.

Notes

Chapter 1

[1] James G. Emerson, *Divorce, the Church, and Remarriage* (Philadelphia: The Westminster Press, 1961), p. 32. Karl Heim quoted in this book from Karl Heim, *Christian Faith and Natural Science* tr. by N. Horton Smith (Harper & Brothers, 1957), p. 28.

[2] Dwight Hervey Small, *The Right to Remarry* (Old Tappan, N.J.: Fleming H. Revell Company, 1977), p. 178.

[3] Victor Pospishil, *Divorce and Remarriage* (New York: Herder and Herder, 1967), p. 49.

[4] G. Edwin Bontrager, *Divorce and the Faithful Church* (Scottdale, Pa.: Herald Press, 1978), p. 131.

[5] Karl Heim, quoted in Emerson, *Divorce, the Church and Remarriage*, p. 32.

[6] R. Lofton Hudson, *'Til Divorce Do Us Part* (New York: Thomas Nelson, Inc., 1974), p. 43.

[7] Paul Eppinger, "A Theology of Divorce," *Single Adults—The Exploding Ministry of the '80s*, workbook prepared by the First Baptist Church of Topeka, Kans., p. 2.

[8] Personal correspondence.

[9] Eppinger, "A Theology of Divorce," p. 12.

[10] Myrna and Robert Kysar, *The Asundered: Biblical Teachings on Divorce and Remarriage* (Atlanta: John Knox Press, 1978), pp. 17-18. Copyright 1978 John Knox Press. Used by permission.

[11] *Ibid.*, p. 31.

[12] *Ibid.*, p. 27.

[13] *Kethuboth* VII:6, cited in Kysar, *The Asundered*, p. 27.

[14] Bontrager, *Divorce and the Faithful Church*, p. 27.

[15] Kysar, *The Asundered*, p. 28.

[16] *Ibid.*, p. 31.

[17] *Ibid.*, p. 54.

[18] *Ibid.*

[19] John Charles Wynn, "Prevailing and Countervailing Trends in the Non-Catholic Churches" in *Divorce and Remarriage in the Catholic Church*, ed. Lawrence G. Wrenn, (Ramsey, N.J.: Paulist Press, 1973), p. 68.

[20] Small, *The Right to Remarry*, p. 177.

[21] Pospishil, *Divorce and Remarriage*, p. 37.

[22]Kysar,*The Asundered*, pp. 56-57.

[23]Robert F. Sinks, "A Theology of Divorce," *Christian Century* (April 20, 1977), p. 379.

[24]Kysar, *The Asundered*, p. 70.

[25]*Ibid.*, pp. 77-83.

[26]*Ibid.*, p. 86.

[27]Richard P. Olson and Carole Della Pia-Terry, *Help for Remarried Couples and Families* (Valley Forge: Judson Press, 1984).

[28]Kysar, *The Asundered*, p. 104.

Chapter 2

[1]William Stephens, "Predictors of Marital Adjustment" in *Reflections on Marriage*, ed. William N. Stephens (New York: Harper & Row, Publishers, Inc., Thomas Y. Crowell, 1968), pp. 119-133.

[2]Paul H. Landis, *Making the Most of Marriage*, Fourth Edition (New York: Appleton-Century-Crofts, 1970), pp. 256 and 341.

[3]Quoted in Gerald R. Leslie, *The Family in Social Context* (New York: Oxford University Press, 1967), p. 643.

[4]Information from a study done by August Hollingshead in 1949-50 in New Haven, Conn.

[5]Lucile Duberman, *The Reconstituted Family: A Study of Remarried Couples and Their Children* (Chicago: Nelson-Hall Publishers, 1975), p. 44.

[6]Bruce Fisher, *When Your Relationship Ends* (Boulder, Colo.: Family Relations Learning Center, 1978), p. ix.

[7]Bruce Fisher, *Rebuilding: When Your Relationship Ends* (San Luis Obispo, Calif.: Impact Publishers, Inc., 1981), p. 18. Copyright © 1981 by Bruce Fisher. Reproduced for Richard P. Olson and Carole Della Pia-Terry by permission of Impact Publishers, Inc., P.O. Box 1094, San Luis Obispo, CA 93406. Further reproduction prohibited.

[8]*Ibid.*, pp. 5-19. These blocks are elaborated in much greater detail through the rest of the book.

[9]*Ibid.*, p. 19.

[10]Neil Simon, *Chapter Two* (New York: Random House, Inc., 1979).

[11]James Emerson, *Divorce, the Church, and Remarriage* (Philadelphia: The Westminster Press, 1961), p. 23.

[12]*Ibid.*, p. 24.

[13]Mel Krantzler, *Learning to Love Again: Beyond Creative Divorce* (New York: Harper & Row, Publishers, Inc., Thomas Y. Crowell, 1977), p. 3.

[14]S. Soul, "Effects of Grief and Personal Adjustment on Remarriage" (Ph.D. diss., University of Oklahoma, 1979).

[15]Krantzler, *Learning to Love Again*, p. 234.

[16]*Ibid*, pp. 234-235.

[17]The Fisher Divorce Adjustment Scale available from Family Relations Learning Center, 450 Ord Drive, Boulder, CO 80303.

[18]See Robert O. Blood, *Marriage*, 2nd ed. (New York: Macmillan, Inc., The Free Press, 1969), pp. 37-61.

[19]Fisher, p. 6.

[20]Emerson, *Divorce, the Church, and Remarriage*, p. 148.

[21]*Ibid.*, p. 53.

[22]*Ibid.*, p. 55.

[23]*Ibid.*, p. 62.

[24]*Ibid.*, p. 69.

[25]*Ibid.*

[26]*Ibid.*, p. 75.

[27]*Ibid.*

Chapter 3

[1]Mordecai L. Brill, Marlene Halpin, and William H. Genne, *Write Your Own Wedding*, (Piscataway, N.J.: New Century Publishers, Inc., 1979), pp. 17-18. Reprinted from WRITE YOUR OWN WEDDING by Brill, Genne, and Halpin © 1979. By Permission of New Century Publishers, Inc. 220 Old New Brunswick Road, Piscataway, New Jersey 08854.

[2]*Ibid.*, p. 19.

[3]*Ibid.*, p. 20.

[4]*Ibid.*, p. 31.

[5]A. B. Hollingshead, "Marital Status and Wedding Behavior," *Marriage and Family Living* (November 1952), p. 311, quoted in Jessie Bernard, *Remarriage: A Study of Marriage* (New York: Russell & Russell, Publishers, 1956, 1971), p. 40.

[6]Susan H. Fields, *Getting Married Again* (New York: Dodd, Mead & Co., 1975).

[7]Marjabelle Young Stewart, *The New Etiquette Guide to Getting Married Again* (New York: Avon Books, 1981). Originally published by St. Martin's Press, Inc. Copyright © 1980 by Marjabelle Young Stewart.

[8]*Ibid.*, p. xiii.

[9]Joseph M. Champlin, *Together for Life*, rev. ed. (Notre Dame, Ind.: Ave Maria Press, 1972).

[10]Gay and David Gilliland-Mallo, personal correspondence.

Chapter 4

[1]Paul Tournier, *The Meaning of Persons* (New York: Harper & Row, Publishers, Inc., 1957), p. 146.

[2]Laura Singer with Barbara Lang Stern, *Stages: The Crises That Shape Your Marriage* (New York: Grosset and Dunlap, Inc., 1980), p. 48.

[3]*Ibid.*, pp. 40-41.

[4]Virginia Satir, *Peoplemaking* (Palo Alto, Calif.: Science and Behavior Books, 1972), p. 135.

[5]Myron R. Chartier, personal correspondence.

[6]Mel Krantzler, *Learning to Love Again: Beyond Creative Divorce* (New York: Harper & Row, Publishers, Inc., Thomas Y. Crowell, 1977), p. 153.

[7]*Ibid.*, pp. 150-153.

[8]Emily B. Visher and John S. Visher, *Stepfamilies: A Guide to Working with Stepparents and Stepchildren* (Secaucus, N.J.: Lyle Stuart, Inc., Citadel Press, 1980), pp. 121-140.

[9]Clifford J. Sager, *et al.*, *Treating the Remarried Family* (New York: Brunner/Mazel., Inc., 1983), pp. 66-72, 355-361.

[10]*Ibid.*, pp. 74-81.

11 Susan M. Campbell, *The Couple's Journey* (San Luis Obispo, Calif.: Impact Publishers, Inc., 1980), pp. 10-15.

12 Gay and David Gilliland-Mallo, personal correspondence.

13 R. Lofton Hudson, *Marital Counseling* (Englewood Cliffs, N. J.: Prentice-Hall, Inc., 1963), p. 24.

Chapter 5

1 Morton M. Hunt, *The World of the Formerly Married* (New York: McGraw-Hill, Inc., 1966), p. 269.

2 J. C. Wynn, *Family Therapy in Pastoral Ministry* (New York: Harper & Row, Publishers, Inc., 1982), pp. 32-47.

3 Emily B. Visher and John S. Visher, *How to Win as a Stepfamily* (New York: Dembner Books, 1982), p. 7.

4 Lucile Duberman, *The Reconstituted Family: A Study of Remarried Couples and Their Children* (Chicago: Nelson-Hall Publishers, 1975), pp. 107-110.

5 Frederick Capaldi and Barbara McRae, *Stepfamilies: A Cooperative Responsibility* (New York: Franklin Watts, Inc., New Viewpoints, 1979), pp. 123-126.

6 Clifford J. Sager, *et al.*, *Treating the Remarried Family* (New York: Brunner/Mazel, Inc., 1983), p. 251. Used by permission.

7 *Ibid*, p. 28.

8 Esther Wald, *The Remarried Family: Challenge and Promise* (New York: Family Service Association of America, 1981), pp. 201-209.

9 Wynn, *Family Therapy in Pastoral Ministry*, p. 37.

10 Sager, *Treating the Remarried Family*, p. 224.

11 Quoted in Emily B. Visher and John S. Visher, *Stepfamilies: A Guide to Working with Stepparents and Stepchildren* (Secaucus, N.J.: Lyle Stuart, Inc., Citadel Press, 1979, 1980), p. 182.

12 Sager, *Treating the Remarried Family*, pp. 116-117.

13 *Ibid*., pp. 362-363.

Chapter 6

1 Gay and David Gilliland-Mallo, personal correspondence.

2 David Dalke, "A Model of Ministry to the Divorce-Caused Single-Parent Family" (D. Min. diss., San Francisco Theology Seminary, 1977), pp. 75-76.

3 Robert E. Elliott, "A Theology of Divorce" (Perkins School of Theology, Dallas, Texas, 1976), p. 11, quoted in Dalke, "A Model of Ministry," p. 110.

4 Suzanne Ramos, *Teaching Your Child to Cope with Crisis* (New York: David McKay Co., Inc., 1975), p. 28, cited in Dalke, "A Model of Ministry," p. 83.

5 Dalke, "A Model of Ministry," p. 83.

6 E. E. Lemasters, quoted in Dalke, "A Model of Ministry," p. 73.

7 Clifford J. Sager, *et al.*, *Treating the Remarried Family* (New York: Brunner/Mazel, Inc., 1983), p. 33.

8 *Ibid*., pp. 341-342.

9 *Ibid*., p. 335.

10 Gay and David Gilliland-Mallo, personal correspondence.

Chapter 7

1 Lloyd Saxton, *The Individual, Marriage, and the Family*, 4th ed. (Belmont, Calif.: Wadsworth, Inc., 1980), pp. 546, 550.